P9-CAM-845

ALL NIGHT, ALL DAY, Angels WATCHING OVER ME

edited by

EVELYN BENCE

A GUIDEPOSTS BOOK

ZondervanPublishingHouse
Grand Rapids, Michigan

A Division of HarperCollinsPublishers

All Night, All Day, Angels Watching Over Me

Copyright © 1995 by Guideposts, Carmel, NY 10512. All rights reserved. No part of this book may be reproduced, stored in a retrieval system or transmitted in any form or by any means, electronic, mechanical, photocopying, recording or otherwise, except for brief quotations in reviews, without the written permission of the publisher. Address inquiries to Rights & Permissions Department, Guideposts, 16 East 34th Street, New York, NY 10016.

First Zondervan edition, 1996

Requests for information should be addressed to:

■ ZondervanPublishingHouse
Grand Rapids, Michigan 49530

Library of Congress Cataloging-in-Publication Data

All night, all day, angels watching over me / edited by Evelyn Bence.
     p. cm.
     This anthology originally published by Guideposts, 1995 containing previously published material.
     "A Guideposts book."
     ISBN: 0-310-21036-4
     1. Angels.   I. Bence, Evelyn, 1952–
BT966.2A45   1996
235'.3—dc 20
                                  CIP
                                          96-7392

Every attempt has been made to credit the sources of copyright material used in this book. If any such acknowledgment has been inadvertently omitted or miscredited, receipt of such information would be appreciated.

Scripture quotations marked (KJV) are from King James or Authorized Version of the Bible.

Scripture quotations marked (RSV) are from the Revised Standard Version of the Bible, copyright 1946, 1952,1971 by the Division of Christian Education of the National Council of the Churches of Christ in the United States of America and are used by permission.

Scripture quotations marked (NKJV) are from The New King James Version of the Bible. Copyright © 1979, 1980, 1982 by Thomas Nelson, Inc., Nashville, TN 37214.

Scripture quotations marked (NIV) are from the Holy Bible, New International Version. Copyright © 1973, 1978, 1984 International Bible Study. Used by permission of Zondervan Bible Publishers.

"A Glimpse of Heaven's Glory" by Janet Fisher is from *Guideposts* magazine. Copyright © 1986 by Guideposts, Carmel, NY 10512.

"Two Minutes to Live" by Dennis T. Jodouin is from *Guideposts* magazine. Copyright © 1987 by Guideposts, Carmel, NY 10512.

"Seeing the Light" by Virginia Sendor is from *Guideposts* magazine. Copyright © 1988 by Guideposts, Carmel, NY 10512.

The English translation of a prayer by Nemesian of Numidia was taken from *Prayers of The Martyrs* compiled by Duane W.H. Arnold. Copyright © 1991 by Duane W.H. Arnold. Used by permission of Zondervan Publishing House.

"This is the Time I Must Sing" words by William J. & Gloria Gaither. Music by William J. Gaither. © Copyright 1975 William J. Gaither. All rights reserved. Used by permission.

This is an original Guideposts book, created and edited by Evelyn Bence.
Designed by José R. Fonfrias
Printed in the United States of America

00 01 02 /❖ DC/ 20 19

Contents

v

PART THREE

Angels Watching... In the Afternoon

PART FOUR

Angels Watching... At Night

Preface

HIS IS A BOOK ABOUT ANGELS. It is a collection of firsthand accounts written by women and men who have been granted a glimpse of these special envoys from heaven. First and foremost, however, it is a book about faith in God, for all of the writers included here are going to tell you about their own spiritual journeys and the effects that angelic visitations have had on them.

"All Night, All Day, Angels Watching Over Me" is a folk song that has been sung around campfires for generations. As the logs sputter and the flames leap into the darkness, the song never fails to remind and reassure that angelic hosts are close at hand. Yet how seldom it is that anyone is permitted to see these hovering, protective beings, or hear them, or even sense their presence. There is a theory about God's purpose in rationing the appearances of His angels: In His desire to gain the attention, and the veneration, of human beings, what better way than to astonish them occasionally—but not too often—with something out of the ordinary.

God's reasons are not to be fathomed, but the fact remains: He does send His angels to earth. And no poor earthling can encounter them without standing in awe of the One Who created them.

You can be sure that God has the full attention of the authors in this book.

They are a varied lot, these writers, most of whom are not writers at all. They are mothers and firemen, prison inmates and women pilots, Christians and Jews—people who have told their stories because they want to share with you the fruits of their astonishment.

The angels you will read about come in different shapes and sizes, just as people do, only more so. At first you might have difficulty recognizing some of them—a voice in the suffocating smoke of a burning building; a guiding light on a stormy night; a kindly woman selling pencils—for they bear little resemblance to the popular concept of angels as serene beings with enormous wings. But turn back for a moment to Bible times:

Put yourself in the sandals of the slave girl Hagar; listen to the voice that startles her as she sits forlornly beside a fountain in the wilderness.

Picture Daniel as he stands on the bank of the Tigris; he looks up to see a person whose face is shooting out blinding flashes like lightning, but all the while the men around him see nothing.

Bring to mind once more the perplexing advice from Hebrews 13:2 about being hospitable to people you don't happen to know: "For thereby some have entertained angels unawares."

There is life-changing stuff to be had in the pages that follow; angels are catalysts of change. There is healing in the experiences of the writers you will come to know. There is courage to be gained, and consolation, and hopeful hints of heaven. And if nothing else, as you close this book you will have a feeling of security that comes from knowing that His angels are watching over you, all night, all day.

∽

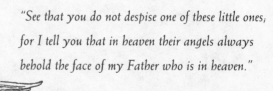

PART ONE

Angels
Watching...
In the Morning

"See that you do not despise one of these little ones;
for I tell you that in heaven their angels always
behold the face of my Father who is in heaven."

—Matthew 18:10 (RSV)

❧ Cheryl Heer ❧

BORN IN 1988, RYAN HEER (pronounced "hare") is a youngster who has good reason to know that angels are real. He's seen them. He can describe them. Once, when given a book with some drawings of angels in it, he picked out certain pictures—ignoring others—as examples of what angels look like: bright yellow skin and curly blond hair; wings and long white robes. He even commented on where the book's illustrator had gone wrong. "Some angels have faces, some don't," he said matter-of-factly. Just how Ryan came to know so much about the subject is something you're going to discover in the story his mother wrote for this volume.

Ryan's mother's name is Cheryl. She and Ryan's dad, Jeffrey Heer, have another son, Jordan, three years younger than Ryan. They are an Indiana family with a long line of Hoosier forebears on both sides, and they live in Fishers, a suburb of Indianapolis. Both Cheryl and Jeff work at the professions they were trained in:

3

Cheryl as a nurse at Community Hospital in Indianapolis, and Jeff as a family counselor. They are a modern, dual-income couple who work as hard at their jobs as they do at parenting. Cheryl puts in ten-hour shifts at the hospital three days a week. Jeff is employed part-time at a mental health center; the rest of the week he sees patients in his private counseling practice. They have it arranged so that one or the other, or both of them, are home for their boys.

Cheryl has chosen to write about the time when her little boy was desperately and frighteningly ill because she wants other people to read, not just about the wonder of angels, but about prayer and its power. She cannot forget the vast network of people who were asking God to watch carefully over Ryan. She is also aware of the good that can come from the sharing of Ryan's story. At the hospital where she spends much of her time in the bone marrow transplant and intensive care unit, she is regularly with patients who are critically ill. Cheryl has had ample opportunity to know, and be thankful for, the sudden, excited glint of reassurance that comes into a dying man's eyes when he hears about Ryan's angels.

As for Ryan himself, his angels have reassured him, too, as you shall see. At this writing, he is in kindergarten, strong, healthy, and learning how to read. He loves baseball and almost anything to do with the sport. Not long ago he saw a movie called *Angels in the Outfield*, which had a lot of California Angels major-leaguers in it.

"When I grow up," Ryan announced firmly after the film was over, "I'm going to play for the Angels."

The way things have turned out, he hasn't had to wait as long as he thought. That's because of the application Ryan made to join one of the fourteen Little League teams in the Hamilton Southeastern school system. One day Coach Rick Lear called up to say Ryan had been accepted. And which team of the fourteen had he been assigned to?

The Angels.

Turn Over Your Eyes

by Cheryl Heer

Hush! my dear, lie still and slumber,
Holy angels guard thy bed!
Heavenly beings without number
Gently falling on thy head.

—Isaac Watts

F IT'S A BOY, what will his name be?" Some couples discuss the possibility for weeks or even months before the birth of their first child. Not
so in our house. Five years before the birth of our first son in September 1988, my husband Jeff and I agreed on a boy's name: Ryan.

Our choice wasn't based on the meaning of the word—"little king"—but on
the personal qualities of a "brother" of mine, Ryan Updike. I say "brother"
because when Ryan was three and I was about eight, he became an unofficial
part of our family; we baby-sat for him evenings when his mother was at work.

Ryan was a high-school junior when tragedy struck: Bone cancer took his
left leg and, too quickly, his life. Yet all through his last painful months here
on earth, Ryan's courage shone brightly. When life got tough, Ryan was
brave and strong. He was at peace with his Creator. His funeral was a celebration. Visitors at the wake heard upbeat rock music in the background.
Right after the funeral church service, hundreds of classmates gathered in

5

the school yard and released colorful helium balloons as a tribute to Ryan.

When I first laid eyes on my own six-pound Ryan, I whispered a prayer of thanksgiving, followed by a request: that God would bless him with Ryan Updike-like courage and strength for as long as he lived on this earth—and "please, Lord, may that be a good, long time."

From the day we brought Ryan home from the hospital, every night Jeff and I have sung "Jesus Loves Me" as we laid him down to bed. Even now, Ryan and his younger brother Jordan will start yawning when they hear the tune. Later, I added two songs to the night repertoire: "There's Just Something about That Name" and Ryan's favorite, "Turn Your Eyes upon Jesus." He calls it "Turn *over* Your Eyes." The first time he asked me to sing the song by that title, I smiled. *Isn't that cute?* I thought. But the more I thought about it, the more clearly I saw that in misquoting the words, he had profoundly expressed their real meaning.

At age three, Ryan, always the serious sort, chose to turn over his heart to Jesus. Having heard prayers addressed to "Father, in heaven"; having heard Bible stories about Jesus, now in heaven; having heard family stories about Ryan Updike, gone to heaven; out of the clear blue Ryan asked me, "How can I go to heaven someday?"

On February 25, 1991, tow-headed Ryan and I snuggled together on our family room couch, and he asked Jesus to come into his heart. I marked the day on the calendar that hangs inside the pantry door. For two years running we've celebrated the day by inviting a few of his friends to a "spiritual birthday" party, complete with candles and a plastic Jesus figurine on Ryan's cupcake.

Ryan's first five years of life were pretty ordinary by our suburban Indianapolis standards: scrapes, bruises, occasional squabbles, sometimes tears, plenty of laughter. With a child's not unusual awareness of death, he occasionally expressed a typical fear of that ultimate separation: "Mommy, I hope you don't go to heaven."

I'd offer typical motherly assurances: "Don't worry, Ryan."

There was even a predictable quality to his coming down with chicken pox in mid-March 1994, close on the heels of his younger brother Jordan's splotchy outbreak. But four days later, I knew something was out of the ordinary. Ryan was throwing up, his fever soaring as high as 106 degrees, and by the hour one pox behind his right ear was noticeably larger, redder, puffier. If I lightly touched it, he cried out in pain. "Ouchy! Ouchy!"

On Tuesday afternoon, March 22, Jeff carried our moaning, rigid Ryan to the car and we drove him to the doctor's. The pediatrician sent us on to an ear-nose-throat specialist. And after a quick examination, he suspected a pox infected with strep-A bacteria. He sent us to the local hospital.

Jeff and I stayed in Ryan's room all night, horrified by the sight: The pox was swelling and spreading like wildfire. Lying on his back on a cooling bag, surrounded by soft pillows, Ryan couldn't hold his head straight; his left cheek rested on his left shoulder. The deadly strep-A infection was ballooning, inching into his face and head and across his shoulders.

By Wednesday evening doctors feared the swelling would block the breathing passages. In an ambulance we were whisked across town to Riley Children's Hospital. Ryan had always thought ambulances were "cool." But now he didn't even notice the lights and sirens that ushered us through the city streets.

Up to this point, I'd been able to maintain some measure of courage, probably bolstered by my toughened professional persona. After all, I'd worked on hospital trauma teams; I currently worked with bone-marrow-transplant patients. But they were other mothers' sons and daughters. This was different. With every bump in the road, Ryan let out a scream that tore my heart. What could I do but hold his hand and pray?

Thursday morning two young doctors drew Jeff and me aside. "Do you have any pictures of Ryan? It would be helpful if we could compare the swollen areas to his normal features."

For a brief second I stared at the residents who had inadvertently broken through the last of my professional defenses. I burst into tears that would not stop. They wanted to know what my son once looked like. The terrible thing about it was, Ryan no longer looked human.

The doctors at Riley did what they could, but Ryan didn't improve. The swelling spread across his back until his head, twice its normal size, sat on his shoulders bolt upright. Highly medicated, he slept most of the time; when he did awaken, his brown eyes were tiny slits in his distorted face.

For the next several days neither Jeff nor I hardly left Ryan's isolation-ward room. Occasionally one of us dozed on a fold-out bed. Mostly I nervously watched the heart monitor, the dripping IV, the pulse oximeter that measured the oxygen in his blood, ready to reach for a buzzer should something not be right. I fretted about whether the doctors knew what they were doing. When visitors arrived or called, I tried to be brave. I thanked friends and family for their kindnesses, their stuffed bears and bunnies, colorful balloons, cheerful cards, and prayers—their own and assurances of heavenly appeals from a number of extended networks.

For myself, my prayers were my tears, like those of the distressed psalmist who asked God to "put my tears into Your bottle" (Psalm 56:8, NKJV).

By the weekend, the doctors were as sober as death. They were talking about spinal cord damage or surgery. And they'd introduced the big "if"—if he survives.

Sunday morning Jeff and I agreed that Jeff should go home to spend a few hours with Jordan. He was at home with my mother who couldn't coax him to eat. I stayed at the hospital and saw Ryan through the day's first torturous physical exam. The oh-so-gentle poking and prodding provoked wails from him that stretched my endurance as tight as his taut skin. And on this morning a new factor further separated me from him: When the doctor woke Ryan, I could no longer see a sliver of his eyes; they were puffed completely shut.

When the doctor left, Ryan fell back into his drugged sleep. I stood for a second at the foot of his bed. The way he was surrounded on all sides by white pillows made me turn away. It looked too much like a coffin.

Trying to distract myself by cleaning up the room, I discovered a book pushed back on the bookshelf under the TV mounted near the ceiling. Jeff had been reading it earlier: *The Men's Devotional Bible*, a New International Version Scripture text supplemented in the margins by 365 daily readings.

The Psalms, I thought, *they've comforted me before. Maybe reading a psalm will calm me down.* With that in mind, I opened to the middle of the book and was skimming a few pages when a headline drew me in—a short devotional written by Billy Graham. It was keyed to Psalm 91:11: "He will command His angels concerning you to guard you in all your ways." Billy Graham's last line spurred my lagging spirit: "Believers, look up, take courage, the angels are nearer than you think."

Thank You, Lord, I prayed. *Forgive my fear. Give me courage. Make me brave. And please, send Your angels with Your healing power.* At that point I became surprisingly specific. *I ask that You send four angels, one in each corner of the room, to guard our Ryan.*

I stepped to Ryan's bedside with a new assurance and strength. Though Ryan didn't respond, I assumed he might be able to hear me. I recited Psalm 91:11 and told him about the angels I'd asked God to send. "The angels are going to watch over you as Jesus heals you, so you can go home." Then for the first time since we'd arrived, I sang him all three of our favorite songs: "Jesus Loves Me," "Turn Your Eyes upon Jesus," then "There's Something about That Name."

There was no evidence of improvement, yet the rest of the day I wasn't quite as compulsive about checking the monitors, not as worried or restless. That evening I was willing to go home and let Jeff sit through the night shift. As soon as I awoke the next morning, I called in, wanting a report of every detail of the doctor's movements, Ryan's movements, the monitors' movements.

An excited Jeff picked up the phone.

"What's up?" I asked. "What's happened?" I couldn't get an answer fast enough.

"You're not going to believe this, but in the night he woke up. He got up on his knees and was crawling around the bed like a dog, rearranging the pillows. I told him to get back and lie down. And he said, 'But it doesn't hurt anymore.' Just to prove it, he lifted his head up off his shoulders."

"What? You're sure? I'll be right there!"

From that moment on, Ryan's condition noticeably improved. When I got to his bedside, I could again see the brown of his eyes. He still had no neck, but there was no question that the swelling was going down. Eager for a demonstration, I said, "Show me what you can do with your neck."

He pulled his head up and forward.

We all broke into laughter. "Oh, Ryan, you look like a turtle," I said, "pulling your head out of its shell. It's your new 'turtle power.' "

I pointed out some of the stuffed animals, cards, and balloons people had sent in. Suddenly I stopped and changed the subject. "Oh, Ryan, I'm so glad you're getting better. Yesterday Mommy sang our songs, and I prayed for angels to be in your room."

"Yeah, I know."

"Did you hear me pray?"

"No."

"Then how do you know?"

"I saw the angels."

I glanced at Jeff. *He saw the angels? Is he talking gibberish?* Our conversation was

10

interrupted by a nurse asking questions and drawing blood. And then doctors, and relatives, and other visitors.

That day Ryan was awake more than asleep. When they changed his sheets, he bravely insisted he wanted to try to get out of bed and sit in a chair—by himself. Within a few days, he was riding the hallway in a red wagon. And ten days later we went for the best ride—back home in our Jeep, stuffed with bears and forty-two balloons. As we pulled onto the road, the bright-eyed Ryan, who now matched our recent family snapshots, heaved a big sigh. I turned toward the backseat and laughed when I heard his hospital good-byes: "It sure feels good to be free."

A few days later Ryan sat on a bench next to my vanity table as I put on my makeup. We were alone and both in the right mood for a serious conversation. "Ryan?"

"Yeah."

"I want to talk to you about something."

"Yeah?"

"I want to ask you about the angels." I was looking straight at him, and he suddenly grew still and sober. "Do you remember you told me you'd seen them?"

"Yes."

"Where were they? How many? Four?"

"They were flying all over the room, lots of them."

"Over your bed?"

"Yes. Everywhere."

"What did they look like?"

"There were little ones like little kids and big ones like big people. They were white and bright yellow like the sun."

"Did they say anything?"

"Yes. They told me Ryan said hi."

"Ryan?"

"Ryan up in heaven."

"The one you're named after?"

"Yes."

"Did they say anything else?"

"They told me that Jesus said He loves me." He was answering my questions but offering no embellishing details.

"Are you sure about this?" I finally asked.

He looked straight into my eyes. "I'm serious, Mom."

At dinner that night I repeated my morning round: "Ryan, tell Daddy about the angels."

His story hadn't changed, and he again grew somber, as if he'd stepped onto holy ground.

Ryan's been home four months now, and I continually thank God for His healing and for the angels He sent to his bedside. Ryan has a heightened awareness of God and heaven and a new gratitude for His watching care. I no longer hear him say things like "I hope you don't go to heaven," for his heavenly talk, and there's plenty of it, is positive: "Heaven must be a nice place....Someday I hope I can play with the angels in heaven....Someday will I be able to fly with the angels?"

And Ryan is passing along his strong belief in angels. But more than that, this confident belief has strengthened his love of his Lord. In June we took Ryan and a neighbor friend to the Indianapolis zoo. Midway between the lions and the bears, I overheard Ryan nudging his friend: "You need to know Jesus, so you can be in heaven with me some day."

The other night as he was getting ready for bed, Ryan told Jeff that the angels sometimes come into his room "and we talk."

"Talk about what?"

"We just talk," he said.

"Do they come every night?

"No. Just sometimes."

On the Fourth of July we sat on the trunk of my parents' Chrysler and watched an impressive display of fireworks. Young Jordan buried his head in my chest. "Scary," he repeated, unsure of the booming thunder. But Ryan? You might say he turned over his eyes to the giant sparklers in the sky.

Waiting for the next act, Ryan posed his burning question: "Do you think angels are watching the fireworks?"

"Yeah, I bet they are," I answered.

He had the last word, himself. "And *I* bet they think they're pretty."

Late in July we threw a party to celebrate Ryan's miraculous recovery. The decor? Angels! I found angel-shaped candy molds, and made yellow angel mints that floated on a whipped cream cloud on top of the white cake. House and lawn furniture weighted down big purple and yellow balloons, each printed with a bold THANK YOU. In the backyard, under a bright blue sky dotted with a few fluffy clouds, family and friends watched as Ryan and his buddies threw water balloons and whished down a wet slide into the swimming pool.

At the end of the exhausting afternoon, Ryan, Jordan, and their cousin Brittany gathered up a few of the helium-filled thank-you balloons. Joyful tears came to my eyes at the culmination of our celebration: Our brave Ryan released his balloons, which ascended straight up over our roof. Till the balls vanished from our sight, Ryan kept his eyes turned over to the heavens, dancing and chanting a new song: "Thank You, Jesus. Thank you, angels."

Janet Fisher

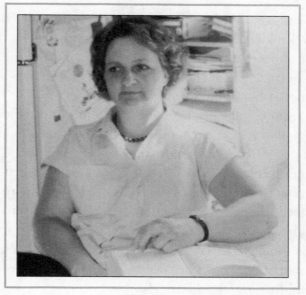

JANET FISHER LIVES WITH HER TWO TEENAGE SONS, Stephen and Joshua, in Salmon, Idaho. That's only sixty miles down the Salmon River from where they used to live in Challis. It's splendid, mountainous country, known for its timber and for its mines. In Salmon, gold is the major industry, with a new mine just starting up; in Challis there's a big molybdenum mine. It's a great area for a holiday if you like to hunt and fish or challenge the white water of the Salmon, which Native Americans have long called "The River of No Return."

Janet herself likes nothing better than to put on a backpack and go hiking in the mountains, though as a single mother and the breadwinner she hasn't had a lot of time for that sort of thing. She has always worked hard to keep her family healthy—and together. Back in Challis she was head cook in the elementary school and would do janitorial cleaning at night. In Salmon she works six days a week at Car Quest, an auto parts store. Sometimes after work she'll get in a bit of baseball or basketball with her boys, though something has been telling her lately that she's not as limber as she once was. On Sundays you'll find her at her church, Faith Bible Chapel.

Moving away from Challis has been, on the whole, a good thing for Janet. She does miss being closer to her mother; she doesn't miss living on an earthquake fault with not infrequent tremors registering from 4 to 4.8 on the Richter scale. Janet has many harsh memories of Challis, worst of all the death of her firstborn, Travis, at the age of six. Yet for all the sad and tragic times she has experienced, she is a woman intact. She has lived through the rough times because of her faith.

"I depend upon God," Janet says, "all the more because I am a single mom. I believe that He will always meet my needs in some way, either through people, or my church, or through His angels."

When Janet talks about Travis, she is serene. That her little boy saw some angels, and that they talked to him, remain for her a stabilizing force. His angels have made her even more confident of her faith in God. But has she herself ever seen an angel?

"A couple of years ago," she says, "I was in a room praying and fasting when I looked up and an angel was standing in the door. He gave me a message, then left. Did I see him or didn't I? I say I did. Did I see him physically or did God open my eyes spiritually at that moment? Angels are always present whether we see them with our physical eyes or not. I feel their presence."

There always comes a day when Janet straps on her backpack and heads out to climb a mountain alone. She has numerous rugged heights nearby to select from—Taylor, McGuire, Ajax, Goldstone. "It makes no difference which one I climb," she says. "The one I choose is always my Mount Sinai."

A Glimpse of Heaven's Glory

by Janet Fisher

"Did you not know that I must be in my Father's house?"

—Luke 2:49 (RSV)

 DON'T KNOW WHY TRAGEDY STRUCK our family that bright October morning. Nor why I, of all people, should have been allowed that glimpse of glory. I only know that a presence greater than human was part of the experience from the beginning.

The strangeness started the evening before, when I allowed six-year-old Travis to play outside past his bedtime. I'd never done this before. Travis' two younger brothers were already asleep in bed, and he should have been, too; he had to go to school in the morning, after all. But Tara, the little girl who lived across the street, was playing outdoors late, too. Though Tara was a year older, there seemed to be a special bond between her and Travis. I heard their happy shouts as they played hide and seek under the enormous stars—just as I used to here in our little mountain town of Challis, Idaho.

And then, later, when I'd called him in at last and he was in his pajamas, he'd suddenly grown so serious....

17

"Mommy?" Travis had finished his prayers as I sat on the edge of his bed. He took his hands and placed them tenderly on my cheeks. Such a solemn little face beneath the freckles!

"What, Babe?" I smiled.

"I...just love you, Mommy," he said, searching my eyes. "I just want you to know that I love you."

The words remained with me as I got ready for bed. Not that it was unusual for Travis to show affection. His outgoing nature had become even more so after he accepted Jesus as his Savior, at age five. Little children who know Jesus seem to bubble over with love for the whole world. It was the intensity—almost the urgency—with which he'd said the words that was unlike him.

As I lay in bed that night, the sense that something out of the ordinary was about to happen stayed with me. Our house is small, and since my mother came to stay with us I've shared a bedroom with the children. I could hear their soft, restful breaths as they slept. That wasn't what kept me awake. Nor was it the empty space beside me—my ex-husband was now married to another. Yes, our family had certainly had its moments of pain, but our faith had brought us this far.

I thought back to that time, four years before, when I'd realized my need for the Savior and invited Him to take over my struggle. How magnificently He had! So much help had been lavished upon us going through the divorce, the changed life-style, the financial difficulties. From our pastor and church friends I'd gained strength and hope. But it was the conversion of the little freckle-faced Travis that brought me the day-by-day lessons.

"Why are you worried, Mommy?" Travis had said so many times, a hint of impatience in his wide brown eyes. "You have Jesus. We'll get the money for that bill." And we always did.

Two A.M. "I love you, Mommy" still pealed in my ears like some distant, gentle bell. I remembered that as my closeness to Jesus increased, my spirit would sometimes hear messages from Him.

I am preparing Travis for something, I'd heard this silent voice tell me, many times. And this did seem to be the case. Hadn't there been that night a couple of months ago…? I'd awakened before daylight and noticed Travis sitting on his bed…just sitting, in the purple predawn.

"What's the matter, Babe?" I had asked him.

"Don't you see them?" He sounded disappointed.

"See what?"

"These two angels."

I breathed in sharply; I saw only the familiar room. The boy was wide awake, perfectly calm. I asked him if he was afraid.

"No, Mommy," he'd said. I waited by his bed a little while. Then he said, "Okay, they're gone. You can go to bed now." That was all. But thinking back on that experience, I felt again that sense of the extraordinary pressing close upon us.

The morning of October 28 dawned bright and still. There was the usual bustle of getting breakfast, finding socks that matched, pencils with erasers and so on. Ten minutes before the time he usually left to walk to school Travis became suddenly agitated:

"Mommy, I've got to go now."

"Babe, it's early. You've got lots of time. Sit down."

"I've got to go now! I've just got to!" Travis cried.

"Why?" I asked in bewilderment. He mumbled something about his teacher, about not being late. It didn't make sense: He was never late. "Wait a few minutes," I insisted. "Finish your cocoa."

"Mommy, please!" To my amazement big tears were rolling down his cheeks.

19

"All right, all right, go ahead," I told him, shaking my head at the commotion. He dashed to the door, a hurrying little figure pulling on a tan jacket. Across the street, little Tara was coming down her walk. I saw the two children meet and set off toward Main Street together.

Five minutes later I was clearing away the breakfast dishes when it happened. A shudder of the floor beneath me, then a hideous screech of writhing wood. There had never been an earthquake in Challis, but I knew we were having an earthquake now. I ran from the house calling over my shoulder, "I've got to get to Travis!"

I was at the driveway when another tremor flung me against the car. I waited till the earth stopped heaving, then climbed into the driver's seat.

I'd gone two blocks when I saw a woman standing beside a pile of rubble on the sidewalk, the debris of a collapsed storefront. The look on her face was one of nightmare horror. Unrolling the window, I was surprised at the calmness of my voice as I asked, "Was someone…caught?"

"Two children," the white face said thinly. "One in a tan jacket…."

I drove swiftly on. Past people running toward the damaged building. Around the corner. To the school. Oh, I knew. I knew already. But maybe (please, God!), maybe farther down the street there'd be two children standing bewildered at a curbside. There were not, of course. I drove back to the rubble heap.

Then a numb blur of events: police, firemen, people struggling with the debris. Identification. Arms around me. I was at the clinic. I was being driven home. I was in my living room again. My mother was there, and I was telling her and my two little boys what had happened. Mother was praying.

Suddenly, as I sat there in the living room, perhaps even in mid-sentence—I don't know how long it took—I was being lifted right out of the room, lifted above it all, high into the sky, and placed by a beautiful gate. A cluster of happy people stood within the gate. In utter amazement I began recognizing the youthful, robust faces: Dad, my favorite aunt, Grandpa…and in the center of them all, the radiant form of Jesus! As I watched, He stretched out His hands to welcome a child who was approaching, a smiling boy dressed in what seemed to be an unbleached muslin tunic over long trousers of the same homespun fabric. Travis ran forward and grasped the hand of Jesus, looking up at Him with eager brown eyes. The cluster of people welcomed my son, and he seemed to recognize them, although some he had never met. As the joyful group turned to leave, Travis suddenly turned his shining face toward me.

"It's really neat here, Mommy."

"I know, Babe." My throat felt choked, and I don't know whether I spoke aloud or not.

"I really like it here."

"I know."

"Mommy…I don't want to go back."

"It's okay, Babe." And it was okay, in that transcendent moment. Nothing I could ever do, nothing that could ever happen here on earth, could make Travis as happy as I saw him right then. When I looked around me, I was back in my home.

That's where the long battle of grief was fought, of course: in the kitchen with its empty chair, in the bedroom where he'd said his good-night prayers, and the yard where he'd played hide-and-seek. Transcendent moments do not last—not for us on earth. Years have passed since the day of the earthquake, passed among the daily routines of cleaning, cooking, chauffeuring, praying.

But neither do such moments fade. That scene at heaven's threshold is as vivid in each detail today as in the measureless instant when I was allowed to see. I have been granted another glimpse since then, this time of Tara among a group of joyfully playing children, all dressed in those tuniclike garments. (I did not see Travis this time, or anyone else I recognized.)

Tara's mother understands no better than I the why of a child's death, the why of heaven's glory. I know only that both are real, and that—when we hear the answer at last—it will start with the words, "I love you."

~ Jerry B. Jenkins ~

JERRY B. JENKINS IS ONE OF THESE PEOPLE who was brought up being told that he had a guardian angel, but since he'd never seen one, or knew anybody who had, he could only accept it by faith. He's still never seen an angel—so far as he knows—but over the years he's become a firm believer in their existence. It started, as you'll see, with an incident that occurred during the morning years of his life. It scared and bewildered him at the time, so much so that for a long while he could not bring himself to tell anybody about it. He didn't want to be thought of as "kooky."

Today Jerry makes his living as a writer. It's likely that an introduction to him is not necessary, because you have read some of his books—there have been more than a hundred of them—and perhaps you know him for his stories in *Reader's Digest*, *The Saturday Evening Post*, or any number of other magazines. Jerry is a former vice president for publishing for the Moody Bible Institute of Chicago; he's still a writer-in-residence there, though he does his writing at home.

The Jenkinses, Jerry and his wife Dianna, live out in the Illinois countryside west of a small town bearing the biblical name of Zion. They call their place "Three Son Acres," and, yes, they do have three sons, Dallas, Chad and Michael, who range in age from early teens to a bare majority. Jerry works in a building next to his house, which contains his office, a garage, a workout room, a batting cage with pitching machine, and even a racquetball court. It should come as no surprise then that Jerry loves sports, altogether fitting for an author whose biographies of Orel Hershiser and Nolan Ryan have made the best-seller list of *The New York Times*. There have been other popular Jenkins biographies of sports figures (Hank Aaron, Walter Payton, Meadowlark Lemon); he has written widely on family issues of marriage and parenting. There have been books of fiction (*Left Behind, Rookie, The Operative*), and he has had the honor of assisting Dr. Billy Graham with his memoirs.

The Black Hole

by *Jerry B. Jenkins*

And out of the darkness came the hands
That reach through nature, molding men.

—Alfred, Lord Tennyson, *In Memoriam*

S A CHILD, one of the highlights of my week was playing tag in the parking lot after church on Sunday nights. We kids would burst from the tiny sanctuary of the Oakwood Bible Church in Kalamazoo, Michigan, and race among the cars in the parking lot.

It wasn't that I didn't take church seriously. Church was a matter of course for us. After all, Sunday was the Lord's day. After breakfast we put on our best clothes and walked the three tree-lined blocks to Sunday school and morning worship. Sunday afternoon we played or read books. This day more than others I might ask Mom or Dad spiritual questions. Deep questions. Like *Can I really know I'm going to heaven?* Or *Do I really have a guardian angel?* My mother assured me that an angel was near me always. *What does the angel look like?* I'd ask. *Is it he or she? Big or little? Old or young?* Mother was like the others in the Oakwood Bible Church milieu; angels were talked about but never seen.

Sunday evening we all walked the sidewalk again, back to the white-frame, picture-postcard church for a less formal service. At night we were allowed to wear sneakers, unless I was singing a solo, which I did on occasion. My premiere was a bold performance of a favorite children's song: "I Met Jesus at the Crossroads."

During the evening sermon I wrote notes to my brothers. We all chewed on the Life Savers Mother kept in her purse. And we waited for the last verse of the last hymn so we could run to the dark parking lot filled with Chevys and Fords for our wild game of tag.

In 1960, when I was ten, I was the youngest and smallest of the Sunday night regular tag players—boys and girls, ages ten to fourteen. My size gave me one advantage: I had a knack for being best able to slip through the crowd and out the door. Once I heard that final amen, I would "walk—don't run" down the back steps, through the foyer, the first to step foot onto the sidewalk. And once I was outside, I ran. The game had begun.

One particular fall night, our family filled a row near the back. So far so good. And I had maneuvered myself a seat at the end of the pew, closest to the door. At the crack of dismissal, I leapt out the aisle, down the stairs, and out into a pitch dark night.

Yes! I made it. No one was even close behind me. By habit I took a hard left, along a sidewalk close to the building, and sprinted with all my might toward the parking lot.

Just past the edge of the building, where the sidewalk ended—wham! An arm as firm as oak caught me in the stomach. My hands and feet flew out ahead of me, but the arm held me upright until I could stand again. Dazed, with my breath slowly coming back, I looked down at a sight I could hardly believe: I was standing, teetering, at the edge of a huge, deep crater.

I staggered back. Then I remembered. The parking lot had been excavated that week. I myself had watched the bulldozer dig the foundation for a new sanctuary. I'd played sidewalk supervisor as Dad and others had slid a truck-load of cinder blocks down a wooden ramp and made piles of them in that hole. I'd helped deliver soft drinks Mom had sent over.

With rubbery legs I slunk toward the church door. By now my friends were out and running, away from the construction site, off to the right and around toward the big backyard. And now I saw the usually empty street lined with the cars that would have been in the parking lot. I was too shaken to join in the play. For a long time I just stood near the front door, thinking about what might have happened. I would have fallen in, would have hit those cinder blocks, been knocked out cold. The night was so dark, no one would have found me until morning. By then it would have been too late. Now my wild imagination took over. I pictured the headlines: *Jenkins Boy Found Dead.*

But the arm that saved my life? Whose arm was it? Big Walt Burke, my Sunday school teacher? With his bulk, he could have stopped me. And he did sometimes hang around outside and warn us kids, including his daughters, to be careful. No. He was just coming out now.

Old Mr. Kemple, the church patriarch who looked the part of a Southern gentleman? But he was too small and frail to have held me back. I would have run him down. And he was still inside.

The truth was I'd been saved by something I couldn't see. By someone I couldn't see. I couldn't explain the mystery and it scared me.

When we got home my older brothers asked what was wrong with me. *Nothing. Leave me alone. Why don't you mind your own business?* If I told them, they would laugh, if not at my reckless stupidity then at my vivid imagination.

I did tell my mother, at least part of the story. "After church I almost fell in the hole," I said. But I couldn't tell her about being caught up short by an invisible arm—that was too spooky to admit. Only as the years went by did I begin to connect that arm at my waist with the guardian angel I had always wondered about. My mother's assurances of divine protection had proven more firm than she had ever imagined.

Today I no longer sing church solos. I no longer leap down the church steps, trying to be the first one out. We don't live within walking distance of our church. I now have sons of my own, and churchgoing has not changed a lot from those years in the sixties at Oakwood Bible. Today, at Village Church in Gurnee, Illinois, with a voice very much like my dad's, I admonish my sons to walk—don't run—inside God's house. If the service runs long, my wife hands breath mints down our row. When they hear the last amen, my boys make a beeline for the back door.

And late at night, I see my boyhood self in my sons, afraid, sometimes, of the dark. When the bogeyman lurks in the bedroom closet or outside the window, I assure them the closet is safe, the windows are secured. As a parent I'll do my best to protect them. As for the things a parent can't see or control, we trust those things to God. Then I tell them my story about the night I almost fell into the black hole. About the arm that held me back from disaster.

I quote from a King James psalm I heard as a child: "For he shall give his angels charge over thee, to keep thee in all thy ways. They shall bear thee up in their hands, lest thou dash thy foot against a stone" (Psalm 91:11-12).

These things, my child, never change.

> *Lord, I would bless you for your ceaseless care,*
> *And all your work from day to day declare!*
> *Is not my life with hourly mercies crowned?*
> *Does not your arm encircle me around?*
>
> —Lucy E.G. Whitmore

Dorothy Nicholas

ONE EARLY MORNING when she was a little girl growing up in a little mountain town in eastern Kentucky, Dorothy Nicholas rubbed the sleep from her eyes and saw an angel standing by her bed. She knew it was an angel because of the intense white light surrounding the stranger she had never seen before.

"Your grandmother is coming for a visit today," the angel told her, then disappeared. Dorothy didn't know what to do with this sudden piece of information. She felt she must tell her mother about it, and yet she hesitated. Even then she knew that her parents thought of her as a "strange" child. Her nose was always in a book and she never really enjoyed the things that the other children in Ransom, Kentucky, liked to do. Dorothy will tell you today that she has always thought of herself as having been "born old."

As it turned out, Dorothy did tell her mother what the angel had said; the result was not unexpected—an angry lecture about her fanciful imagination and how she'd better stop reading "all those fairy-tale books." Still, later that day Dorothy was sitting in the one-room Blackberry Creek School next to her house when her Grandmother Hatfield came driving up from West Virginia in her grandpa's Model T. Vindication, however, was not all that sweet. It only made her mother angrier; Dorothy was warned never, ever, to say a word to anybody about what had happened or "people will say that the little Smith girl is touched in the head." From that time on Dorothy buried the memory of the angel's visit deep in her mind until the events in the story you are about to read brought it to the surface again.

Dorothy's story takes place a long time ago in Barboursville, West Virginia, a town of two thousand inhabitants. She lived there during the twenty-five years of her marriage to Walter Peyton, the father of her two children, Donna and Walter Michael. Her husband was employed on the railroad and she worked steadily as a licensed practical nurse. She liked to write, too, gaining some measure of success for her stories, and especially, she says, "as a contest writer for short slogans."

It was as a mother that Dorothy felt her greatest fulfillment. She and Walt took in more than thirty foster children, as many as four or five at a time. The children would come, stay a while, then go. She never knew where they went because, by law, foster parents were never told. Ever after, when Dorothy's been out shopping or driving through the county, she's had what she calls the "sweet sadness" of wondering if she might not be passing one of her grown-up babies.

The bitter sadness, the bitterest of all, came one night in October 1981. Her son Mike, grown up by then and working in Florida, was walking home from a convenience store when he was robbed and murdered by a twenty-one-year old man on drugs.

Dorothy has moved around a lot in her lifetime. Her marriage to Walt ended in divorce in 1965. By then her children were off on their own and, though she was a grandmother three times over, it didn't stop her from doing something she'd always dreamed about—college. She enrolled in Marshall College (now University) in Huntington, West Virginia, and for three years she majored in English with a minor in social studies. But there was still something else she wanted to do—travel. She figured that as a nurse she could pick up employment almost anywhere, and off she went. While working at St. Francis Hospital in Miami Beach, she met Fred Nicholas. It just so happened that he, too, liked to travel, and since he was in the dry cleaning business and could find a job almost anywhere that people needed clean clothes, off he and Dorothy went—as man and wife.

They moved from one place to another every year or so until, after Dorothy's serious case of embolism and later a stroke, they returned to Barboursville and hung up a sign: "Journey's End." Dorothy has never recovered fully and is frequently housebound, but when she can she writes about past adventures, including the one offered here. This is not the only angelic encounter she can recall. She believes she has had over twenty such visitations in her seventy-two years. "Often," she says, "in my room at night, I'll feel something beside my bed and I'll look and see an angel in a fragile white dress with flowers in her hair."

The angel you are about to meet is not like the messenger of Dorothy's childhood or the delicate being of her later years. Beyond the profound effect it had on her, this angel suggests two things to Dorothy: that God has a wonderful sense of timing and a great sense of humor. "After all," she asks, "can you really picture an angel doing diapers?"

She Came Selling Pencils

by Dorothy Nicholas

Mercy now, O Lord, I plead
In this hour of utter need;
Turn me not away unblest;
Calm my anguish into rest.

—Alexander Clark

Y HUSBAND WALT was employed as a foreman for the Chesapeake and Ohio railroad. But in his spare time he built us a house, first a small, white-framed house four miles outside the village of Barboursville, West Virginia. Then another, bigger, in town. Shaded by big willow trees and a Christmasy blue spruce. With neighbors on either side.

In 1958, after our daughter Donna had left home and married and our son Michael was eleven, Walt and I took in three foster children, all babies under a year old. All boys, not brothers. Greg, Larry, and Johnny lay in cribs lining three walls of a first-floor bedroom. For a season I cared for them as if they were my own—chicks safe under my mother-hen wings.

I spent my days changing and laundering cotton diapers, mixing formula and scrubbing bottles. I made time for cradling and rocking, even as I kept Walt and Michael well-fed and happy.

In 1958 my "clothes dryer" had no electrical wires. The moving parts? My back and arms. Pinch clothespins. And windblown cord ropes—five or six strung between crossbars in the backyard.

One May morning I could hardly hang up a load of diapers, the sun hurt my eyes so badly. A few minutes later, washing my hands in the bathroom sink, I discovered that the problem wasn't the bright sky. In the mirror I read the horrifying sign on my red, blotched face: measles.

Hadn't Mama told me I had nothing to worry about—as a child, I'd had every manner of measles?

I thanked God this was the short—and light—variety. With three babies to take care of, I couldn't afford to be ill. But for just three days, I could manage. Walt pitched in when he got home in the evenings. After school, Michael was old enough to warm a baby's bottle and change diapers. And my sister Lorraine, who lived three miles away, stopped in so I could rest a few times throughout the day.

But I was not to get off that easily. After a few days of relative health, I knew something was drastically wrong. A fever raged. I felt sick all over. A goiter-like swelling developed under my chin.

With my medical training, we weren't the kind to call a doctor for every sniffle. But it didn't take Walt long to summon Dr. Curry, who in those days made house calls. He shook his head: I was very sick. I'd need an IV, a catheter, complete bed rest.

My mind was clear enough to be concerned about one thing—or maybe three in one—the babies. *What will we do about the babies? If I'm too sick for too long, the county will take them.*

As if reading my thoughts, Dr. Curry said I could stay at home, not go to the hospital, if I obeyed his orders. Complete bed rest meant I wasn't to put weight on my feet, for any reason. He'd visit me once a day. His nurse would come twice.

Lorraine, bless her, came to my rescue. For days she arrived at seven in the morning, after she'd made breakfast and school lunches for her own brood. She was tuckered out at the end of a day, yet stayed until Walt got home from work, even cooked his dinner.

Late one afternoon, after Lorraine had emptied the diaper pail and left, the phone rang. After a short conversation, Walt walked the few steps from the living room to our bedroom where I was firmly planted in bed. Tenants in the house we still owned four miles out of town said their electric pump was down.

"Do you think you'll be all right if I go out and see if I can get it started? Mike will be here."

I knew the world couldn't stop because I was sick. Someone else's family had no water. Of course he had to go. "Yes, the babies are asleep. I'll be okay with Mike around."

I heard Walt give clear instructions to Mike: "I've got to go down to the other house for about an hour. You stay in the front yard, so you can hear your mother if she calls out the window."

An hour passed and Walt didn't return. Everything was under control until one of the babies, then another, then all three woke up. From the room next to mine, I heard rustling and then whimpering and soon a trio of wails.

No need to worry, I told myself. *Bottles will keep them quiet for a while. Mike can warm the milk and prop up the bottles.* I craned my neck to yell out the open window at the head of my bed. "Mike…oh, Michael. Come here. I need you."

Silence. No "I'm coming." No "just a minute." No sound of a bouncing ball or a humming boy.

I tried again. "Michael. Are you there? Michael!"

I was talking to the air. He'd done this before, forgotten an instruction and gone off with a friend who'd come by and proposed some exploit. He'd be back soon.

Every few minutes I called out the window. If he couldn't hear me, he could surely hear the babies crying. Still no response.

I kept an eye on the clock. I listened to my three squalling babies for ten or fifteen minutes. It's not a sound a *healthy* mother can tolerate for long, and I was far from healthy. Yet the doctor's warnings had been emphatic and stern. I was not to get out of that bed. I *couldn't* get out of bed, tied as I was to all these medical tubes.

Lord, I need some help with the babies. Bring Mike home. Or Walt. Or a neighbor. Yes, maybe a neighbor will drop by.

I'd no sooner thought the word *neighbor*, when I heard a light knock on the front door. I glanced out the window but couldn't quite strain far enough to see who might be standing on the stoop. "Come in," I called.

The screen door squeaked open and closed. I listened as someone stepped through the living room and into the hallway leading to the bedrooms. There at my doorway peered a plump, gray-haired woman about five-foot-two. I'd never seen her before, but she looked the part of a grandmother who must be new or visiting in town.

She wore a flowered cotton housedress, her lap covered by a blue and white gingham apron with deep pockets. Even then her hairdo was old-fashioned: parted perfectly in the middle, pulled straight back from her face in a tight bun. "Hello," she said pleasantly.

"I'm glad to see you," I said. "I'm alone right now, and…" I stated the obvious, "the babies are crying."

"Maybe I can look in on them," she offered, turning her head toward the raucous noises.

"Oh, please," I asked with some relief. In 1958, in Barboursville, West Virginia, with about two thousand households, nobody thought about being suspicious of "granny" strangers wearing round, wire-rimmed glasses. "They need bottles, and they're probably wet," I said.

I listened carefully as she went down the hall to the nursery. Things calmed down a little as she announced her presence with a motherly cooing and clucking. *Good, she's changing their diapers.*

In a few minutes she was back at my door. "Yes, I think they're hungry. What did you say about bottles?"

In the refrigerator she found the bottles Lorraine had filled. With a farmer's match she lit a gas burner and warmed the milk.

I suggested she prop the bottles so all the boys could feed themselves and then come sit and chat.

She pulled up the overstuffed chair. "You're new in the neighborhood?" I asked.

"I live around," she said vaguely.

"And what's your name?"

As if to change the subject, she reached into an apron pocket and pulled out a handful of bright yellow pencils. "I'm selling pencils. Do you need any?"

"I'm not sure I have any money," I replied. "My son is always coming to me for school money. My purse is over there on the end of the dresser. If you'd just hand it to me, I'll look and see."

She ignored my request and laid the whole handful of pencils on my bed-side table. "You can have these," she said. "I really don't need money anyhow."

What a strange thing to say, I thought. *If she doesn't need money, why is she peddling pencils?* Door-to-door selling of such a low-cost item was not a wealthy woman's trade. *And what kind of person doesn't need money?*

Worried that she'd think badly of my family for leaving me alone, I explained my plight. My sudden sickness. The tenants without water. My son who had apparently wandered off.

"Oh, I met the boy going off on his bicycle as I came into the yard," she responded. "A nice-looking boy, but he needs to learn to be more responsible. You need to work on that."

Who is this stranger telling me how to raise my son? I wondered. But conversation quickly turned to my ill health. Periodically she'd get up and check on the babies, now quiet and content.

After maybe a half an hour she got a little fidgety, as if she wanted to leave. "When do you think your husband will be coming home?" she said.

"Any minute now," I said hopefully. He should have been back already. "But if you need to leave, please, don't feel you need to stay with me. If you'll just give me your address, I'll have my husband stop by your place tomorrow and leave the money for the pencils. And for your help, thank you so much."

"You're most welcome," she said, "but I'm not going until he gets here."

It was probably fifteen minutes before I heard Walt's pickup pull into the driveway. "He's here now," I said eagerly.

She quickly got up, turned, and said, "I'll be going now since he's here."

"No, no," I protested. "Wait just a minute so he can pay you for the pencils."

Without saying another word, she walked out of sight, through the living room, across the kitchen linoleum, and out the back door. Just as my husband came in the front door.

In a second he was at the bedroom doorway. "Quick," I greeted him. "Go out the back door and overtake the lady who *just* left. I owe her some money. You'll see her. She can't be out of the yard yet."

Walt did as I asked, and in about ten minutes he returned, looking perplexed. "There was no lady in the yard, Dorothy. And I looked all around in the street and went halfway down the next block. Didn't see anyone. What's this all about, anyway? And where's Mike?"

I told him my story.

Well before dark Mike jumped off his bike and let it fall in the front yard. He let the screen door slam behind him and bounded through the house.

"Young man, where have you been?" Walt asked. Yes, he'd found an adventure with a friend who had lured him to the ballpark. From my room I heard Walt's stern kitchen-table lecture about manhood and responsibility.

Later, before he went to bed, I asked Mike about the lady he'd met in the yard. With adolescent bewilderment, he said, "Lady? What lady? I didn't see any lady."

But it was obvious to us all that *someone* had changed three wet diapers, plopped in the otherwise empty diaper pail. And *someone* had fed the boys' bottles, now empty in the kitchen sink.

The doctor's stay-at-home remedy ultimately didn't work. The swelling on my neck grew hot and red; on Memorial Day I underwent emergency surgery. The diagnosis: acute thyroiditis, a rare side effect of measles.

The few days I was in the hospital Lorraine took full responsibility for Greg, Larry, and Johnny; they remained in our care until they were adopted.

In early June, when I was back on my feet, I set out on a personal campaign to find the lady selling pencils. Surely she had to have knocked on other doors. Had a new family moved to town? Had someone's mother-in-law come to stay? I inquired at the grocery store, the doctor's office, the church and school, the woman's club, the library and restaurants. No one had seen the granny in wire-rimmed glasses, with gray hair bunned and parted down the middle.

No one had been sold any pencils. Especially like the nine that lay on my night stand. Yellow, perfectly round, not hexagonal. And perfectly blank, with no lettering, not even a black numeral 2.

For years I kept those pencils in a desk drawer. (You might know how it is with children and grandchildren in and out. Always needing something to write with. One by one the pencils "walked off," and one day they were all gone.) Occasionally I'd pick them up and gaze at them, trying to fathom their mystery. I could come to only one conclusion: I had asked God for help and He had sent a grandmother angel to tend the babies in my care. Yet when I think of God sending one of His pristine angels to change dirty diapers, well, I want to start laughing. What a sense of humor.

And the bit about selling pencils? Only God knows what it means. You never know when an angel steps in.

Write Your blessed Name, O Lord, upon my heart, there to remain so indelibly engraved, that no prosperity, no adversity shall ever move me from Your love. Be to me a strong tower of defense, a comforter in tribulation, a deliverer in distress, a very present help in trouble, and a guide to heaven through the many temptations and dangers of this life.

—Thomas à Kempis

～ Pat Egan Dexter ～

IF YOU EVER FLY into Sky Harbor Airport in Phoenix, Arizona, you might find that it's one of the days when Pat Egan Dexter is there. Check out the airport's interfaith chapel and see if you don't come upon someone who looks like the woman whose picture is on this page. She'll be dressed simply in black and white, with a cross pinned to her blouse, and, as a member of the Dominican Family Laity, she'll be conducting a Catholic communion service.

What?

Can this grandmotherly woman (six grandchildren) be the same person who was once Patricia Egan, the naughtiest, sassiest little girl in her grade-school class? That's what they called her at St. Mel's on the west side of Chicago. The nuns had their hands full with this child who was regularly late for daily mass, who never listened, who had a habit of rolling her eyes in consternation at almost anything she was told to do, and who, since she was a charity student, should have been better behaved. Could this be the same individual who, when warned by a frazzled nun that she might be destined for hell, dared to reply with an impudent, "If you are what goes to heaven, I'm not interested in going there"?

Yes, this is the same Pat Egan who was sent to the basement of the convent for punishment. And, yes, this is the same person who wondered about the nun she met down there, the one who did all the laundry and worked so very hard and so very long—how could that drudge be such a happy woman?

The basement laundry at St. Mel's became the starting point for Pat's spiritual pilgrimage. That's where a kind and patient nun known only as "Sister Laundry" taught a hungry, little girl about God's love. Pat doesn't mention Sister Laundry in the story you will read here, but then there are a lot of things she doesn't mention that would be nice to know about Pat.

She doesn't tell you that the man she married, Ralph Dexter, was her bosses' boss when she worked for the State of Arizona as an assistant to the computer manager (she was courted, it seems, on State time), or what a wonderful husband and father Ralph has been.

She doesn't tell you what a nightmare it was living on the little farm that Ralph took her to outside Mesa. Meeting cows, horses, and goats face-to-face was not the romantic picture that this Chicago city girl had of country living. The first time Ralph picked up a squawking chicken and handed it to her she screamed, petrified with fear. Nor does she tell you how really bad it was when the pesticides from the commercial farms around then caused her years of suffering before the cause was discovered.

She doesn't tell about how marrying Ralph meant that she could be a home-making mother with time for volunteer teaching and the writing she wanted to do. Her published books speak for the success she's had: three works of fiction for teenagers involving and solving the problems they face as children of divorce and of alcoholic parents. Her third book, *The Boy Who Snuck In*, is based on a real boy who did sneak in—though he didn't realize he'd always been welcome—when Pat was directing a vacation Bible school at St. Simon and Jude Church in Phoenix. Lately Pat has been writing books that are curriculum tools on prayer and creative educational techniques for teachers of middle-schoolers. These days, as always, her family comes first, then comes all the work to be done with her Dominican family.

Now that you know a bit more about Pat Egan Dexter, it's time to catch up with her on the pilgrimage that began a long time ago in Chicago. She's about to describe some angels that appeared along the way. They remain the most significant proof of God's love that she could ever tell you about.

God Shows Favor

by Pat Egan Dexter

My soul waits for the Lord
more than watchmen wait for the morning,
more than watchmen wait for the morning....
Put your hope in the Lord,
for with the Lord is unfailing love....

—Psalm 130:6-7 (NIV)

N JANUARY 1956 I walked out of Saint Mary of Nazareth Hospital in Chicago with a smile and a bundle of blue flannel. God had answered my prayers and given us a son. We named him John, after his paternal grandfather. The name has special meaning, "God shows favor." And I had no idea how dramatically that favor would be shown.

Three years earlier God had given us a healthy daughter. I'd had trouble conceiving then and more troubles this second time. Late in the pregnancy the doctor discovered that I was anemic. Yet the baby seemed healthy. And this one a boy, like the brothers I'd grown up with! I welcomed John into our home with a deep gratitude for God's grace.

But just ten weeks later, I carried the baby back into Saint Mary of Nazareth Hospital. He'd contracted measles, which brought on pneumonia, then double pneumonia. He got through those bouts, and came home only to have asthma close in on his lungs until he gasped for breath. I'd awake in the night, always listening in his room for a wheezy rhythm, always terrified I might hear nothing at all. If his breathing was too labored, I'd wrap him in blankets and trek to the hospital again.

One day a doctor in a white coat shook his head and said, "He seems to have an impaired immune system. We have some medication that will help, but...these children rarely survive." We already knew how allergic he was to so many otherwise helpful drugs.

My husband was strangely and stubbornly absent when sickness struck. As a child he had struggled with health problems, and he found it difficult to cope with the doctors and hospital problems that our son's illness entailed. It was a deep-seated emotional thing that I tried to understand. Employed at a hotel, he'd often spend the nights there. That's where he was the rainy spring night in 1958 when Johnny began to gasp for air so desperately that I knew he needed help. I left our daughter Carla with a friend and called a cab. My own coping skills had abandoned me; I was too unnerved to drive down Division Street to the hospital.

The white coats whisked a blue-lipped Johnny out of my arms, away from my reach, into a sterilized room pumped full of oxygen. "O God, please," I prayed. "O God, have You forsaken me?"

Through a large plate-glass window, I watched the doctors and nurses hover over one, then another, of the four cribs in the room. Three sets of parents and I took turns standing at that window. All seven of us waited for good news. All four of the toddlers had equally critical pneumonia. None of us took comfort in the severe eyes of the nursery staff. The nurses kept shaking their heads as if something were terribly wrong.

It was. Early in the evening the head pediatrician walked out of the oxygenated room. He took a deep breath of Chicago's real air and turned to talk to one set of the parents. Then another. Then the third. I don't know exactly what he said, but each mother reached for her husband for solace.

Finally the doctor stood before me. "Call your husband to come and be with you," he said. "You will need him. I'm afraid your boy won't last the night."

Paralyzed, I stared at him.

"Please don't wait," he said. "There is little time." With that, he walked away and left me standing there alone.

I didn't have the strength to explain to the doctor my husband's aversion to being in a hospital. I knew he would not come, even if I begged him. I telephoned my mother, but even as I did, I knew that she couldn't come. She had a sick husband and other responsibilities that tied her to her house. And, anyway, she didn't drive an automobile.

I looked around the stark waiting room. Long wooden benches lining the walls at the end of a long hallway. No magazines. No coffee. No distracting jigsaw puzzle. I saw three couples tenderly comforting each other's sorrow. I began to cry.

Was this the favor God was showing me? Through a window I'd watch my son die tonight. When they'd given up on him, I'd face the doctor's words all by myself.

God, please don't leave me alone this night. I'm so scared. I don't know if I can make it through.

Within minutes of my prayer, I heard down the hall a familiar sound from my years in parochial schools. It was the rhythmic clink of a nun's rosary beads, wooden marbles hung in loops from a rope around a sister's waist. In school there was no such thing as a nun sneaking up on you. The sound of those rosary beads announced her presence as if she wore a bell.

Sure enough, a tall, heavy, tough-looking nun walked into the room. She wore the traditional black habit and white apron. Her face was framed in a white band that covered half her forehead. Her hair, if she had any, was veiled in black. And the chained and grained wooden beads dangled down below her knees.

I froze. This woman reminded me of all the stern nuns who had scolded me into learning algebra and religion. As a rule, the nuns and I had not been on friendly terms. One seemed to go out of her way to remind me of our family's charity status, receiving free tuition and uniforms. For years I had wished I had the power to get away from under their harsh routines.

And now one of "them" had found me here. Tonight of all nights. And wouldn't you know? She sat beside me on the hard bench. What stern message would she have for me?

With a rustle of all that cloth and those beads, she put her arm around my shoulders.

I didn't pull away.

She whispered in my left ear. "God has heard your prayers. You will not be alone this night."

There was comfort in her voice. I looked at her face. Close up, the stern eyes turned gentle. She kept her arm around me. After a while, I leaned into that weighty bosom.

An hour dragged by. When I cried, she pulled a tissue from a pocket and dried my tears. When the tissue was soaked and in shreds, she lifted her apron and wiped my face with the soft cotton. At least once I found myself wiping my nose with her apron.

We prayed together. I'd walk to the window so I could get a good look at John in the crib closest to the glass. The sister stood with me. Nothing changed. The blue lips. His pale, gray skin. His shallow breathing. The nurse still wasn't smiling as she adjusted tubes and held thermometers.

"It's kind of you to stay with me," I finally said. "What's your name?"

"My name is Sister Mary Margaret," she answered. The voice remained gentle. "And I work here."

Maybe she likes the night shift, I thought as the evening took its last breaths.

She continued, "I want to tell you now that I believe your son will live. God has answered yes to all our prayers."

How does she know? She's trying to be nice. She wants me to feel better, bless her. But I don't believe it.

She rubbed my cheek, and I leaned my weight back into hers. It was so nice to have a warm, caring body to snuggle, as did the strangers across the room.

Finally, Sister Mary Margaret gave a reason for her hope: "I see the angels floating above the children's cribs. And whenever I see an angel floating above the bed, I know the child will live. They always have. Tonight all four will live."

I looked at her face again, full of grace. I still didn't believe her, but I could *hope*. Maybe she was right and the doctor was wrong. She smiled at me.

I didn't sleep a wink that night. And Sister Mary Margaret didn't leave my side.

I don't know what time it was. But at one point the doctor nearly ran from one crib to the next, to the next. The stir in the nursery spread to us parents, gaping through that window. *What's happening?* The nurse called for more help. Another nurse and doctor arrived. They pulled out stethoscopes. Shone lights into groggy eyes.

My breath steamed the glass when I saw the doctor raise his head and smile. A nurse nodded to another. The second doctor continued to check a baby near the back of the room.

Aware of our keen interest, a big-capped, big-boned nurse came out and blurted her news to all of us: "Something's going on!" she exclaimed. "There's been a change. *All* the children are getting better! Their lungs are clearing... the...I can't explain. It looks very hopeful."

Sister Mary Margaret still stood at my side. She hugged me. "Believe it," she said. "Your son will live. And he will never be sick like this again."

I hugged her back. With her song of hope in my ears, I believed it could be true.

When the first light of morning came, the night shift went home. They came and gave us another report. The children were out of danger. We parents needed our rest. Everything would be all right if we left and got some sleep.

Even Sister Mary Margaret had to go. "Will you be all right now?" she asked me.

"Yes, I'll be fine. But I want to stay a little longer."

She stood and smiled down on me. Then she turned and walked out of sight.

Such kindness, goodness, I mused as I listened to the clicking rosary beads. *Wouldn't it be wonderful to be that close to God—to be able to put your arms around someone and ease her pain?* The clink, clink of the wooden balls grew fainter and fainter as she walked down the long hospital hall.

A few days later I wrapped a happy, healthy Johnny in a blanket and took him home to our maple-lined street on the northwest side of town. With every passing hour, my hope and faith grew. Maybe I would never again walk into that emergency room carrying a blue-lipped son.

We'd been home nearly ten days before I remembered that I had not even said "thank you" to Sister Mary Margaret. *Hadn't those school-teacher nuns taught me anything about gratitude?* I called the hospital. I reached the switchboard and asked to speak with Sister Mary Margaret.

"There's no nun by that name in the directory," the operator insisted.

I held my ground. "Yes, she does work at Saint Mary of Nazareth. She spent the night with me a few weeks ago. In the nursery unit."

"Let me connect you with the nursery." Was she just trying to get me off the line to answer the next call?

A woman answered the phone in pediatrics.

I tried again. "Could I please speak with Sister Mary Margaret? Would she be 'on' today?"

"Sorry, no one by that name works here."

"I know she does. She told me." My mission seemed very important by this time.

"Just a minute. I'll connect you with the supervisor."

I waited a minute, or more, and repeated my request.

"Sister Mary Margaret?" the supervisor asked.

Finally, someone seemed to recognize the name.

"Could you describe her? Just where did you see her? And when?"

I told her everything. "And I didn't get a chance to thank her for staying with me, for telling me about the angels over the cribs."

There was an odd silence on the other end of the line. Neither confirmation nor denial of the sister's presence. Then the supervisor said, "We used to have a nun with that name. She fits your description, and she worked in the nursery." She paused. "But she died ten years ago."

"She couldn't have! This was two weeks ago." My protests were useless.

The supervisor laughed. "I'm glad you told me your story. It's good to hear that Mary Marg is still around helping out."

When I hung up the phone, I gulped. Sister Mary Margaret had spoken with such certainty. Her gentleness had belied my expectations of her. She had seen an angel attending my baby. Had I dried my tears and wiped my nose on the apron of an angel in a black and white habit?

I had to find a tissue to dry my own tears of joy and gratitude. Like Mary of Nazareth, I pondered God's ways and kept them close to my motherly heart.

It was a long time before I told anyone the story, and recounting the events of that miracle night still makes me cry. God used it to root a deep faith in my once doubting spirit; God's love was personal and for *me*. My encounter with Sister Mary Margaret changed my life. From that day to this, in gratitude I have set my heart on being faithful to God.

That night *was* the last time I rushed John to the hospital with breathing problems. It was as if an angel flipped a switch from "off" to "on" in his immune system. The men in the white coats never could explain it. "One of the lucky ones," they said of John.

Gradually, not unexpectedly, our marriage ended and my husband simply disappeared from view. John was eight at the time of the divorce. He became my stalwart little man who liked to tell me that he would always be there for me. I think he was the one person who really was.

Carla was ten then, and it was she whose illness brought about a major change for us. Carla had a terrible problem with asthma, and the attacks grew so severe that the three of us packed our bags and moved to Arizona where she could benefit from the dry, clean air.

Arizona turned out to be our land of brightness. Carla's health improved; I got a job; I met and married Ralph Dexter and in time we had a son, David. I smile when I think of how John adored his stepfather. Actually, John was the one who went to Ralph and said, "I want you to be my daddy," and it was Ralph who suggested that John ask me if I'd marry Ralph!

The years went by, the kids grew up, John left home and married. There were plenty of good years, then came the bad ones. When we were living on a two-and-a-half acre farm, I began to have trouble breathing. There were long periods in which I was gasping for breath as desperately as my little baby had done back in the hospital in Chicago. For a while I even lost eighty percent of my hearing from a swelling in the Eustachian tube. We moved away from the farm and only then did I begin to recover. It was slow going.

In the meantime, Ralph was diagnosed with cancer. Lymphoma. In 1987 nothing was right: the cancer; every four hours I spent twenty minutes on a breathing machine; even John's marriage was in trouble. One night, in despair I flung myself on the bed in my workroom, an office of sorts. I knew God existed. In my head I knew He loved me, but He felt so far away.

My questions sounded like those of Gideon in the Old Testament. When an angel sat down next to him and said, "The Lord is with you," Gideon responded skeptically, "But sir, if the Lord is with us, why has all this happened to us? Where are all his wonders...? The Lord has abandoned us" (Judges 6:13, NIV).

Still wide awake, holding my head in my hands, at 2:30 A.M., I jumped at the sound of a tap on my window. I turned and heard a loud whisper. "It's me, Mom. I'm coming in." No question. The voice was John's.

Barefoot and bathrobed I walked to the front door and turned the key. On the other side of the door stood the boy who said he'd always be there for me.

"What are you doing here?"

"I knew you needed me. Mom, we've got to talk."

Back in my workroom, I sat on the edge of the bed. He pulled up the straight chair as if he had been given a task to set me straight. And his clear, simple message hit straight to the heart: "Mom, you're going to be okay."

Like Sister Mary Margaret, he stayed until morning, his words and presence giving me the strength to face the dawn and its new day. And to this day I have the strength that my son willed me in the depths of a dark night. I use that strength to love and care for Ralph who goes on—precariously, but he *goes on*. I use that strength to love my God, for ever since that night I've wanted to draw still closer to God, to serve Him more, to show Him my gratitude.

Since 1958, when Sister Mary Margaret saw an angel hovering over my baby's crib, I've continually asked one question: What does being faithful to God mean? What does it mean in terms of me? And in my spirit I sensed a clear direction: to religious sisterhood.

With my family responsibilities, becoming a full-fledged nun was out of the question. Nevertheless, in October 1994, I was received into the Dominican Family as Laity. As laypeople we work with the friars and sisters. We are committed to pray at specific times every day. We meet together regularly to study the Scriptures and writings of the saints. We spend hours each month feeding the poor, visiting prisoners, writing letters for people who can't. And at my local parish I've recently been trained as a grief counselor.

As Sister Mary Margaret walked down the hospital hall away from me, I wondered at her ability to personify God's love in the midst of pain. And now I wonder at the favor He has shown me, granting me the strength and opportunity to do the same for others, putting my arms around young women in pain—offering comfort and assurance of God's love and care.

I like to think that the seed of this ministry was planted by Sister Mary Margaret, whoever, whatever she was, and the angel she saw hovering over my baby's crib.

PART TWO

Angels Watching... At Noon

Rejoice, O young man, in your youth,
and let your heart cheer you in the days
of your youth; walk in the ways
of your heart and the sight of your eyes.
But know that for all these things
God will bring you into judgment.

—*Ecclesiastes 11:9 (RSV)*

∼ Mel Goebel ∼

PRISONER 28138—IN TELLING HIS STORY, Mel Goebel could have used that as a pseudonym instead of his real name. The pseudonym would have been genuine. Convicted on a charge of burglary in 1971, Mel served time in the Nebraska State Penitentiary. How he got there is all too familiar stuff in this day and age: a ninth-grade school dropout; a truck-driver father who was never home; a drunken mother; wrong crowd, alcohol, drugs, burglary, prison. Familiar stuff, and yet....

Years later you'll find that things have not changed altogether for Mel Goebel. He is often back in prison—many prisons. He goes into them as Director of Network for Life, a Christian ministry of Prison Fellowship. Reaching out to prisoners and ex-prisoners is now his full-time job, as well as the chosen mission of his life. It is varied work, much of it person to person, much of it administrative, arranging conferences, creating pilot projects. Often he gathers together teams of ex-prisoners and they go back behind the walls and talk to inmates about the way to find real freedom. Mel is particularly interested in what he calls after-care; he's writing a book about his experiences to convey how critical transition from prison to a local church is.

What are the things that have changed for the old Prisoner 28138? The school dropout now has a bachelor of science degree from the University of Nebraska. He has been married since 1978. In 1987 Governor Kerry granted him a full pardon. He and his wife Jane live in Monument, Colorado; they have no children. Jane helps Mel in his ministry whenever she can, but this is not always possible for her. She has multiple sclerosis, a calamity that Mel and Jane are fighting together, medically and with deep prayer. They are asking for the prayers of others, yours as well.

Mel's father died—as a Christian—in 1992, and his mother, well, that is a story in itself; it will not be told here, except to say this: While you are reading "The Presence," keep in mind that during the time that Mel was in prison, his mother stopped drinking. There was not a day that she did not get down on her knees to pray that her lost son would also be found.

August 21, 1976, will be a memorable date for Mel Goebel. It marks the occasion when he walked out of the Nebraska State Penitentiary.

The Presence

by Mel Goebel

"I tell you, there is rejoicing in the presence of the angels of God over one sinner who repents."

—Luke 15:10 (NIV)

HE IRON GATES of the Nebraska State Penitentiary clanged shut. I sat in the police cruiser, caged, a wire screen separating me from the officers in the front seat. My wrists were handcuffed in my lap; my ankles shackled.

I was twenty-one years old, and angry.

My lawyer had assured me I wouldn't get more than one year— for burglary. Wrong!

My girlfriend had assured me she'd love me forever. When I needed her, she was gone.

My family? What can I say? These days they call it "dysfunctional." A truck-driver dad who was never there, a mother who drank. Seven of us kids floundering.

Flanked by security guards, I shuffled into the ancient, stone fortress. *If I'm going to survive in here, my skin's got to be as thick as these castle walls,* I thought. *These cons in here are pros. I've got to be tough.* And with the mortar of anger, I bricked around myself an invisible wall and called it courage.

An officer handed me an officially approved set of clothes, each piece stamped with my prisoner number: 28138.

There was a rhythm to the prison day: At 6:00 A.M. a wake-up siren blared through the three-tiered cellhouse. By seven an officer flipped a switch that automatically unlocked the doors to the four-man cells. Time for breakfast and then a morning shift of "hard labor": in the winter deep-freeze or under the summer sun, pushing a wheelbarrow full of concrete chunks to a grinder that churned out road gravel. We came in for a morning head-count and lunch, and then we were back outside for an afternoon shift. For each workday I earned twenty-five cents.

After two years of this day-to-day routine I found that my courage and tough-guy image had paid off. I had gained some respect on the premises. I knew how to glare and stare—and fight if provoked. As a weight lifter in the gym, I could hold my own. I could pump two hundred pounds. I also knew how to wheel and deal, and have outside contacts, visitors who would slip me cash, and you could always get some staff person to exchange money for drugs. Then I had street friends willing to drop off drugs, trash that prisoners working the road crews would "innocently" pick up and smuggle in.

That's what my buddy Rick was good at. And then there was Dave. The three of us drug pals knew our way around. Only once was I busted for drugs. I served several weeks in solitary when an officer's search unearthed a quarter pound of marijuana I'd hidden in my pants.

By 1975 my security clearance had been lowered; I slept in a dorm housing a hundred fifty men, six cots to a room. No more wake-up sirens; no all-night lockdown. This dorm was as dank as a pigpen. When it rained an inch of water ran across the floor. With long-handled squeegees we'd push it down a flight of stairs and out the door.

One morning I sat in the yard when a load of new prisoners stepped off a bus. *They're just kids,* I thought. And I was all of twenty-four.

There was a slogan written across the back of one guy's khaki jacket: "Smile, Jesus is your friend." *Is that guy nuts or what? He'll be torn apart in here.*

All the same, that slogan affected me in some odd way. I knew who Jesus was—or who He was supposed to be. As a kid I'd gone to mass and recited prayers I still knew by rote. But God was something remote, distant, and Jesus was unreal to me.

I took a good look at the kid. Later I found him in the prison yard. "Tell me what you know about your friend Jesus," I sneered.

"I'll tell you this," Fred said, looking me straight in the eye. "Jesus Christ *is* your friend whether you like Him or not. He is real and He gives me peace of mind. He'll give you that too—and joy."

I stared at him and walked away. A nut. Yet for several days his words burned into my mind. Those words about Jesus being real bothered me. How did this guy know that He was real? What did he know that I didn't?

About three days later I found Fred in the cell house. I asked him a lot of questions. I was stumbling around, hunting for answers to things that seemed to have no answers. What about the suffering in the world? How come I've had to go through all this pain? Things like that.

Fred had one quick response for all of them. "You have to read the Bible and come to grips with these questions yourself." Though his answer was unsatisfying, it was the right thing to tell me. It sent me to the chapel; I borrowed a Bible and for about three months I attended a Bible study led by two businessmen who befriended me. They came back every week. They acted as if they cared about me. They opened their Bibles and pointed out a story about a loving heavenly Father Who longed for His sons to come home.

I could see myself in the Prodigal Son parable—a kid who'd made a mess of

61

his life, an angry, bitter kid who could easily spend the rest of his life sitting in a pigpen, or a kid who could stand up, turn around, and step in a new direction.

But if I start a new life, who would I be? If I let go of the anger, what will take its place? If I'm not the 'old Mel,' who am I?

On March 16, 1975, I awoke early. Before I'd even opened my eyes I was aware of a something beside my bed. I opened my eyes and at that instant blaring, bright light penetrated my being. I felt an indescribable joy. I shook my head. It was like the joy Fred had talked about, but I could not have recognized it if it had not been inside me, as it was now. In the next bed over, Dave was still dreaming off the joints we'd smoked the night before. My other cellmates weren't up yet.

I got up out of bed and walked to the sink at the end of the room. *I'll get the sleep out of my eyes,* I thought. *Then I'll get my senses.* But each splash of water I threw on my face sent a news flash through my mind: *Today is the day. Today is the day. Today is the day.* While this thought was flashing through my head, I sensed that somebody was standing near me.

I looked over my shoulder. I looked in the mirror. There was no one there. But there was. Something or someone I could not touch or see—a presence. *I've got to get alone,* I thought, knowing I was ready to explode with emotion.

I walked into the hallway, stared out a barred window onto the yard, and started talking to God, daring to address Him as my Father: *I know You've sent someone to usher me in—home,* I prayed silently. I quickly headed down the dorm corridor to the one toilet that provided the privacy of a shower curtain. Even there I wasn't alone. The presence just grew stronger; it was as if the Prodigal Son's Father was opening His arms and enfolding me. I knew at last that Jesus was what I'd always wondered about: He was real. I wept out a prayer of repentance for my sin and rebellion. *God, if You can take my life and do something with it, I give it to You.*

In that earthly setting, an otherworldly love broke through; I felt as if some-one had handed me my release papers from prison, the prison I'd walled up around myself. I reached out and accepted my freedom.

I stayed in that bathroom a long time. After my cellmates had gone to breakfast, I pulled back the curtain and faced the world. I instinctively knew what my prayer had meant. Still flanked by the presence, I headed straight for another toilet—where I had hidden my stash of marijuana. I unscrewed the two bolts at the base of the ceramic bowl, slipped the stuff out, and flushed it away.

My next destination was the chapel, which was down a set of stairs, on the other side of a stony corridor as dark as a dungeon. Halfway down that hall-way I met Dave, coming back from breakfast. I grabbed hold of him and began to rattle on wildly at him. "God came to me this morning....I've given my life to Jesus....God sent me something…I don't know, an angel maybe…and I flushed the marijuana down the toilet."

I could never have imagined Dave's response. Standing there with his back against the wall, he closed his eyes, his knees buckled, and he slid down to the cold, stone floor.

"Dave! Dave! Come on! Get up." He had fainted.

I yanked him up by his armpits. For a quick moment, my overriding feeling was fear. What if a guard came along? He might think I'd knocked Dave out. This was the kind of thing that could get you sent to solitary.

Dave came to. "What's going on? Are you all right?" Dave couldn't answer at first. He tried to tell me about something he saw but didn't see, a thing he could only sense, feel.

"Mel," he said, grabbing my arm, "there's a look on your face. Your eyes. You're different, Mel. You've been with God."

For the next day or two Dave watched me closely. He didn't know how to act with me. Though he wouldn't admit to fainting dead away, he spread the word about what I'd done with the pot. That was beyond his comprehension. "If you knew you couldn't smoke the dope, why didn't you just give it to me? Why did you have to flush it down the toilet?"

We talked for hours. "Dave," I said at one point, "you know that 'thing' you mentioned, that presence you could only sense?" Dave nodded. "Well, it's here now. I can't see it either, but it has stayed beside me. It's my own invisible angel, my prison angel. I believe my angel came to bring me home to the Father." Later that week, sitting facing each other on our beds, I prayed with Dave, who came to God, drawn by the changes he'd seen in me.

Those changes in my life were pretty drastic and called for a new kind of courage. Above my bed, I dotted the ugly institutional green paint with slips of paper on which I'd written out Bible verses. I not only walked away from drugs—buying, selling, and using—but I also quit smoking cigarettes and started running six miles a day. When I walked in the yard, I'd carry a Bible and would strike up conversations about God's power to transform a life.

News of the change in me spread, even to Rick, confined in solitary at the time. About three weeks after my change of life, I was sitting on a small island of grass in the prison yard reading my Bible when I saw Rick, just free from his lockdown.

With a skeptical edge to his voice he said, "What's this I hear? You're a Jesus freak?"

The old Mel would have challenged such a comment. Not anymore. I wanted him to get the story straight, and I didn't care *what* he thought of me. "Rick, can you spare a minute? I want to tell you what happened."

Under a bright spring sun, I told him too about my prison angel and the changes in my life. I read him the first verses of John, "In the beginning was the Word, and the Word was with God….The light shines in the darkness, but the darkness has not understood it....To those who believed in his name, he gave the right to become children of God" (John 1:1, 5, 12, NIV).

As I talked Rick began to cry. "I want what you have," he said.

"All we have to do is pray," I answered, and then and there Rick gave his life to Christ; along with the angels in heaven, I rejoiced that a new brother had been welcomed home.

My new strength was tested many times, very dramatically about a year later when Rick, Dave, and I were known as three of the Christian leaders in the prison.

One morning a teary-eyed eighteen-year-old named Rocky stood at the door of my dorm room and asked if he could talk to me. He'd been in the pen about two months. I didn't know him well, though I had invited him several times to our Bible study.

He quickly explained his predicament. When he'd first come to the pen, he'd accepted a carton of cigarettes and some pot from older, seasoned prisoners. Now some of those guys wanted to collect payment in sexual favors. Rocky was in a corner and wanted advice.

This was a hard one to figure. I asked if we had a little time so we could pray and weigh the alternatives.

Within a day or two Rick and I and a few other Christians had scraped together enough money out of our prison wages to buy a carton of cigarettes at the commissary. Then I went to the gym looking for the leader of the pack, one big, tough guy whom I had never wished to mess with, under any circumstances. We found him, surrounded as usual by four of his loyal gang, ready to defend their own. I walked toward them and held out the carton of cigarettes. "Here's the carton Rocky owes you," I said. "I never collected the two cigarettes of pot you owed me, so the debt is canceled."

I was challenged. "Who do you think you are, telling us what to do?"

My heart pounded in my chest, but I didn't back down. "Because of Christ, Rocky's my brother," I said with a shaky voice. "I have to help him."

I turned my back and walked away, thoroughly expecting that I'd be jumped.

I wasn't.

But within five minutes, the leader of the pack found me in the yard, giving a report to Dave and Rick. Now he was surrounded by seven or eight toughs egging for a fight.

Rick quietly quoted a Scripture: "The servant is not greater than the Master." I understood his meaning: If Jesus had been bruised and battered, I should be willing to take a beating for my faith. I knew I had other options. I knew people who would fight with me and for me. No. That was the old Mel.

The new Mel stood tall without a clenched heart. When he was a pace in front of me, he said, "I don't think I like what you did down there." His chin inched closer to my nose.

I looked him in the eye and called him by name. "If you were threatened, I would do the same thing for you."

With that he turned and walked away, his cohorts in tow.

Dave, Rick, and I knew we'd been a part of the great scheme of love, of God's goodness overcoming evil. I'd memorized a Scripture verse I quickly quoted to my brothers: "Greater is he that is in [me,] than he that is in the world" (1 John 4:4, KJV).

"That prison angel is still hanging around," said Rick.

Amen, I agreed.

For months that gang leader neither hassled nor befriended me; he ignored me. But in time he would acknowledge my greetings and even chat as we passed each other in the yard. The respect I'd tried so hard to earn by acting tough, I actually earned by showing love.

Before I was released from prison in August 1976, the still-unseen prison angel again stood at my bedside, this time at 4:00 A.M. Even in the noisy prison dorm, I was a sound, dead-to-the-world sleeper. But this night I awoke with a start and knew the angel was there and beckoning me to get out of bed to quench an unusually strong thirst. Not understanding the real purpose of my mission, I shuffled to the drinking fountain at the end of the corridor, right next to a desk manned by Officer Powell, a veteran guard, maybe sixty years old.

When I got near him, I knew something was wrong. I'd never seen this man so depressed. He propped up his head with his hands and just stared into space. A long drink at the fountain quenched my thirst and cleared my head. "How are you doing, Officer?" I asked. My angel still at my side, I took the liberty of sitting on the corner of the desk.

"Not so good, Goebel," he answered. "Troubles at home. My wife is leaving me."

As we sat there, my mind briefly flashed back to the day I'd stepped onto the penitentiary grounds, shackled hand and foot, angry at the world. I felt so far removed from the old Mel who had glared at the officer handing me a regulation khaki pants and shirt. That Mel couldn't have imagined the possibility of this encounter, offering to pray with a security officer, any security guard, to say nothing of one who was older than my own parents. What's more, Officer Powell wouldn't have dared let his guard down with the Old Mel. And he couldn't have opened his heart even to the new Mel at any time other than 4:00 A.M., when the corridor of the prison dorm was deserted, men snoring the night away.

From cryptic conversations in the next few weeks, I got the impression that Officer Powell and his wife worked things out. "We're talking again. Things are looking better," he said.

Thank You, Father, I said, aware for sure now that I had a mission for my life both in prison and out. My prison angel was part of it too, for "he" (as I think of him) was always there, just as he is now, whenever I need him.

Frances Mullen Elliott

ON VALENTINE'S DAY, 1994, Frances Elliott's mother, Anne Hendricks, gave her a copy of *Angels Among Us*, a book published by Guideposts containing a number of stories about God's messengers.

"Turn to page 31," Mrs. Hendricks advised, "I think you'll find it interesting." Frances did as her mother said, found a story called "The White Dog," and she did find it interesting. Her mother knew that Frances had experienced her own strange encounter with a dog that left a profound and lasting impression on her—not a white dog, a very large black one.

One of the curious things about Frances and her history with dogs is that once, long before the time she writes about, she was bitten by one. Her family was living in Philadelphia then, before they moved to South Carolina, and Frances was a little girl. The attack was not a vicious one, and she suffered no serious physical injury, yet it gave the child such a terrible scare that she was always wary when any strange dog came near.

When you read her story, you're going to wonder if the dog Frances writes about is an angel. She doesn't say it is. She does say, however, that "There is no doubt in my mind that God has given His angels charge over me." God's protection, His guiding Hand, the affirmation of His presence, these become the theme for the story she is about to tell, not just as it relates to a black dog, but for the unfolding adventures of her life. They fit together like pieces of a puzzle, all part of the whole of her life story.

Frances is a serious-minded, deep-thinking woman who has a strong academic background. At Clemson University she majored in psychology with a double minor in religion and philosophy. She received a master's degree in art therapy from the University of Louisville. She has always been interested in children's education, especially during the years when she volunteered, and was later employed at, Shriner's Hospital for Crippled Children in Greenville, South Carolina.

For a year after her marriage to David Elliott, Frances continued to work, but when their daughter, Aubrey Anne, came along, she decided that she would concentrate on "keeping the home fires burning." David is a civil engineer, a graduate of The Citadel in Charleston, and the son of a minister. Frances and David both teach a children's class at Holmes Memorial Church not far from their home in Greenville.

Are You Running Beside Me?

by Frances Mullen Elliott

Angels, where'er we go,
Attend our steps whate'er betide.
With watchful care their charge defend,
and evil turn aside.

—Charles Wesley

RIGHT AT EYE LEVEL, in front of the exercise treadmill in the play-room, I've posted a Bible verse: "I do not run like a man running aimlessly" (1 Corinthians 9:26, NIV).

Ever since junior high, when I walked down a church aisle and committed my life to Christ, Scripture has played a big role in my life. I've read it. Repeated it. Memorized it. Certain verses speak to certain life situations or seasons. This verse about running has had significant meaning for me for a very long time. It reminds me—and my husband David—to fix our eyes on God's purposes and plans, not on our own.

Admittedly, I like to run. I've been jogging for twenty years, from the days when I was a cheerleader at Parker High School here in Greenville, South Carolina. From my sophomore year on—and all through college—I dated Rusty Dimsdale, a star basketball player who ran track to prepare for his game.

When I graduated from Clemson University in the spring of 1978, I didn't actually have a diamond ring. Yet I was sure that in God's good time I would marry my kind-hearted Rusty, probably after I finished graduate school to qualify as a children's art therapist.

To get started toward this career goal, I'd volunteered one summer to work in recreational therapy at Shriners Hospital for Crippled Children. The kids captured my heart. After I earned a degree in psychology, I took a full-time job at Shriners, to earn money to pay for graduate school.

At the end of my day shift, Rusty's little 1974 MGB would be waiting on the semicircular drive in front of the main entrance. As I went off duty, I'd rush past the glass door and give him my "I'll be right there" sign: a raised index finger that said "just a minute." Actually, it was more like ten minutes. Even if I was running late, I always said goodnight to the children on both the boys' and girls' wards—before I greeted Rusty's sweet grin.

We'd often head for Furman University, where I would jog; he would ride his bike nearby, usually at my side.

But in November 1979 Rusty died. He was killed in the fiery crash of a small commuter plane. In faith I chose to hold on to a verse of Scripture: Isaiah 43:2-3, "When thou walkest through the fire, thou shalt not be burned; neither shall the flame kindle upon thee. For I am the Lord thy God" (KJV).

I'd previously marked the passage in my Bible, and now the words sustained my days. Though Rusty's body was burned, the flames couldn't touch his spirit, at peace with his Lord. Nor could they touch mine, comforted by the Lord, the trustworthy God of the universe.

A few days after Rusty's funeral I was back at work. My body functioned— organizing activities, cookouts, crafts, and games for the children. But my spirit was heavy with grief and confusion. I'd been so trusting and hopeful that Rusty would be at my side until death parted us, when we were old and gray. Not now, in the prime of life.

I missed Rusty most when I walked out of the hospital at the end of the day. He wasn't there in the driver's seat of that mustard-gold MGB. Sometimes, alone, I stopped at Furman to jog. As I ran to release emotion not touched by the physical exertion, I silently recited Scripture.

That was my plan one evening early that next summer. At Shriners I changed into shorts and running shoes. I walked to the parking lot and scrunched down into the MGB that was now mine. Not ready to let go of memories and distressed to see Rusty's car shut away in a dark garage, I had asked his parents if I could buy it.

I drove the four miles to Furman. Toward the end of the long drive shrouded by shrubbery, I slowed down at the sight of the university's green carpet of welcome: a grassy oval surrounding a distinctive fountain just inside the wrought-iron gates. I parked on the oval, right where it intersected the entrance drive. It's common knowledge that the paved road around the oval is a one-mile run. With only summer classes in session, I had the track completely to myself. It was near dusk, but—not to worry— if I took it at a pretty good pace, I could get in one lap before dark. I locked the car, placed the keys in my shoe purse, and set out, around the first big bend, in front of the music building, then toward the science hall.

When I rounded the first bend and my back was no longer to my car, I was alarmed with what I saw out of the corner of my eye: an old, beat-up car had pulled in. Parked directly in front of mine. Two white, disheveled men leaned against the driver's side of their car.

Who knows what they were discussing, but I was convinced of one thing: These strangers were up to no good. They weren't student types; they weren't jogging types. What *were* they doing here—besides watching me? And, as unusual as it was, *no one* else was in sight, pedestrian or driver. *If only Rusty were here....*

But my apprehension and my wish were quickly crowded out by a verse: "What time I am afraid, I will trust in thee" (Psalm 56:3, KJV).

Thank you, Lord. I shifted my mind into a trust-God gear, even as I started calculating my next moves. I was less than halfway around the circle; if I turned around and headed straight for my car, that would be the wrong thing to do. I needed the distance.

No, I would keep running and give the men time to move along.

If I kept running, toward the gymnasium, I could try the door and go inside until I felt safe.

No. The gym was locked, seemingly deserted. And there wasn't a soul in the parking lot on the far side of the gym.

By now the two men, one short, one very tall, had shifted closer to my car, their backsides against their car's back fender.

They're waiting for me. O God, help, I whispered. But as the fear built up inside me, I fervently recited a familiar psalm as if it were a prayer: "The Lord is my shepherd; I shall not want. He maketh me to lie down in green pastures; He leadeth me beside the still waters. He restoreth my soul: He leadeth me in the paths of righteousness for His name's sake. Yea, though I walk through the valley of the shadow of death, *I will fear no evil: for thou art with me;* Thy rod and Thy staff they comfort me...." (Psalm 23:1-4, KJV).

As I quoted the Shepherd's Psalm, all the way to the final "I will dwell in house of the Lord for ever," a huge black dog bounded toward me from the shrubs between the gym and the parking lot. I'd been bitten by a strange dog as a child, and suddenly I felt a surge of my old fear. But this dog was not attacking. He rushed up and fell in stride with me. It was as if we'd been running companions for years; without verbal communication—commands or barks—we ran side by side around the end loop. The dog seemed to have a clear aim and purpose: to stay at my side. And stay with me he did. My courage was strengthened as we came to my car.

As the men watched, I unlocked the door, jumped in, and slammed the door behind me. When I looked out through the window, the dog was gone. Vanished. Right then and there I didn't pause to contemplate the mystery. I just wanted to get out of there. I stabbed the key in the ignition and pushed the start button—a quirky feature Rusty had installed.

I didn't immediately think of the dog as a supernatural messenger, yet I drove off that campus knowing the Spirit of God had guarded me. I could feel His unseen presence in the car. The Spirit was so big and my car so small that I thought the metal hinges and seams might break. God had protected me, I knew, by sending the dog. He had assured me, visibly, that my trust was firmly founded; I had reason to fear no evil—because He was running beside me.

Driving home to my mother's house, I assured God that I would not make light of His protection: I never again would take risks and jog alone at dusk. I also reaffirmed my commitment to "run with perseverance the race" of trust and hope that God had "marked out" for me (Hebrews 12:1)—whatever that might be.

As planned, I left town for graduate school. Whenever I got in a tight corner, the memory of that large black dog increased my faith; it served as proof that God was still running beside me.

I graduated in 1982, trusting God for the right job. My first choice was as an art therapist with children in an orthopedic hospital. After interviewing in several states, I accepted another job back in Greenville, working outside a hospital setting at first. It wasn't the job I had in mind. But my faith and focus on God and His good will never wavered. In his scheme this job was right for me for that time in my life.

Settling into a routine in Greenville, I socialized with old friends, but I had no real interest in dating. Perhaps I was not truly trusting the affections of my fragile heart to God. What about Psalm 56:3: "What time I am afraid, I will trust in thee"? On this count I said, *Someday, Lord. Not just yet.*

I picked up running at Furman, often with Rusty's neighborhood friend, Charlie Butler, a policeman. One day Charlie's sweet mother called me to ask a "favor."

"Frances, can I give your phone number to a nice young man who works with the youth group at my church?" She knew I worked with my church's youth group—and her premise was that we could help each other out.

Despite my reluctance and refusals to other matchmakers, I couldn't say no to Mrs. Butler's genteel frankness. "Oh, Mrs. Butler, since it's you, you may give it to him but to no one else," I joked. It was unlike her to make such a request—and it was unlike me to give such permission.

Early in September I got a call from David Elliott, who asked if I'd have dinner with him.

Dinner? It felt too much like a date. As much as I liked the sound of his deep bass voice—very much the businessman—I kindly said no, I'm sorry.

Undaunted, he asked if I would go to a youth-group Bible study he led at his house.

That I could handle. And afterward—surprise—we went out to dinner!

In the next year I spent a lot of time with this gentle man, who in some ways reminded me of the dog who had quietly picked up my stride and confidently escorted me as if we'd been running companions for years. Our commitment grew, though neither of us tried to define the relationship. David seemed to know that words would scare me away.

The next summer, in the middle of a downpour that aborted a relaxing boat ride and picnic, David pulled roses out from under the seat of his boat, brought them to me in the cab of his truck, and quoted Scripture: "Rise up, my love, my fair one, and come away. For, lo, the winter is past, the rain is over and gone; The flowers appear on the earth; the time of the singing of birds is come, and the voice of the turtle is heard in our land" (Song of Solomon 2:10-12, KJV).

It wasn't immediately obvious, but I soon understood that "my fair one… come away" was David's idea of a romantic marriage proposal.

And I was ready for singing birds. The winter of my grief and confusion was passing. In quiet and in confidence, David—and God's Spirit—had broken through with the new life of spring.

David and I married on August 20, 1983. For several years the two of us continued to jog. But a few years after our daughter, Aubrey Anne, was born in 1989, we bought an indoor treadmill on which we run and track our miles.

Indoors or out, it doesn't matter; I can still use my running time to quote Scripture. And there on a shelf in front of my gaze is a model steam engine, and in the window of that train I see the card on which I wrote my running theme verse: "I do not run like a man running aimlessly."

Winded and wishing back my breath, I often stare at the verse and recount the times I've stayed the course of trust in the present and faith for the future because God sent his guardians to run beside me. Guardians seen or unseen. Guardians heavenly or human. Even a guardian *canis mysterious.*

> *Clothe me, clothe me with yourself, eternal truth, so that I*
> *may run this mortal life with true obedience, and with the*
> *light of your most holy faith.*
> —Catherine of Sienna

77

Peter Fetridge

"HERE AM I, LORD, SEND ME," is Peter Fetridge's prayer at the end of the personal journey he is about to take you on. His life has not been an easy or tidy one, as you shall see, particularly when he describes his own physical pain and his late wife's mental illness. Yet Peter is a survivor, and a grateful one. "Send me" is how he shows his gratitude.

An electrical engineer, now retired, he lives alone in Arlington, Virginia. His income is the monthly check from Social Security, but his outgo is the day-in, day-out work he does for others, especially in the field of his most passionate interest, mental illness.

"I do everything I can to replace people's fears of this affliction with understanding," he says. He serves on the Episcopal Diocese of Virginia Committee on Mental Illness. He belongs to Samaritan's Heart, a monthly prayer and support group for those living with, or touched by, mental illness. He's out often with tapes that show what churches can do for the mentally ill.

Then there is his regular volunteer work at St. Michael's Episcopal Church, and on Wednesday evenings you'll always find him leading a prayer service at the local Oak Spring Retirement Residence. With all these activities there isn't much time left over, though when he can he likes to go fishing with his son who lives only thirty-five miles away in Leesburg.

The words *here am I, send me*, spoken to God by the prophet Isaiah as six-winged seraphs hovered overhead, have become a spiritual touchstone for Peter. They were said at a time of cleansing and commitment for the prophet, a turning point. There was such a time in Peter's life too, but no six-winged seraphim were hovering in his hospital room on that occasion—only a man he had never seen before who came to give Peter a crucial and timely message about suffering pain.

The Healing Message

by Peter Fetridge

Send from the heavens
Raphael thine archangel,
health-bringer blessed,
aiding every sufferer,
that, in thy service,
he may wisely guide us,
healing and blessing.

—St. Rabanus Maurus

S A YOUNG MAN, I was a hunter and fisher. In fact, I'd converted a whole upstairs room in our Rockville, Maryland, Cape Cod house into an outdoorsman's office. There I kept my poles and tackle, my boots and caps, my guns. And that's where I headed one Sunday afternoon in May 1961—the day that would change my life forever.

I was thirty-two years old. Husband and father of a two- year-old son. A homeowner. An electrical engineer and a government contractor. You'd think these reasons and more would have been enough for me to welcome each new day.

But life had turned bitter when my body had been wracked with one, then another, and another, grand mal seizure. Medication helped control them, but the neurologist was talking the possibility of brain tumor, surgery, paralysis. Hints of such a prognosis drove me to despair. I wanted to die.

Deep in my spirit I ultimately wanted to "be there" for my son. But not as a father who couldn't teach his boy how to hunt. Not as a man who would grow old feeling invalid in every sense of the word. Sensing I was heading for an encounter with my Maker, I sought consolation in two disparate sources, first and unfortunately, alcohol. But my despair also prompted me to buy a Bible, which I hadn't read since the grammar school days when I'd sung in a High Church Episcopal boys' choir. That spring I combed the pages of Scripture searching for something, maybe for a reason to stay alive, maybe for permission to take my own life.

That Sunday afternoon, while my wife was out shopping, I walked upstairs contemplating a dark plan for some future day. Listening to subtle, deathly messages, I posed a question: *If I were to kill myself, how would I do it?*

I looked at the four weapons in my gun rack, hung high on the wall, out of any child's reach. There was the Enfield .306 rifle. No. Too long and unwieldy. The Stevens shotgun. No.

Ah, the 30-30 Winchester carbine. A short barrel and lightweight. The previous fall I'd carried it, trudging through the woods of western Virginia. Though I'd shot at a buck, I hadn't got one. At the end of deer season, I'd put the empty rifle back, the top gun on the rack, with a hunter's high hopes for next year.

But maybe it would serve me well before deer season. *Let me check this out*, I thought as I reached with two hands, one on the barrel, the other grabbing the receiver. That's when something went wrong. High above my head, I lost my grip and accidentally cocked the rifle's hammer. Not to worry; all the chambers were empty.

But then, at chest level, my thumb slipped off the hammer which hit the firing pin.

I heard the blast and smelled my own burnt flesh. I dropped the gun and fell to the floor, writhing in pain, rolling in blood. A bullet silent in the "empty" chamber had blasted through my abdomen and large intestines.

My brother-in-law, a houseguest, bounded up the steps and quickly called an ambulance. Other images blur in my memory, but one remains: In the midst of the crisis, I heard my son crawling up the hardwood staircase, obviously distressed, calling, "Daddy, Daddy."

Actually, much of the next ten days is hard for me to recall. Doctors removed burnt flesh and part of my colon. Surgery showed my vital organs had not been hit. Even so, the close-range impact had wreaked havoc. The gunpowder had burned away the skin and muscle covering my stomach. With many abdominal blood vessels damaged, my heart enlarged. Within days, a staph infection settled in. Within a week, gangrene.

A critically high fever combined with massive doses of drugs caused what I can only describe as hallucinations from hell. I don't remember details of the delirium, only an overriding horror. And still I wanted to die. If this was life, I wanted out.

My room was closely monitored. Isolation. Even visitors—my wife and sister only—wore green gowns and caps and face masks as they stood helplessly over my bed.

Maybe four times a day nurses walked in carrying instruments of torture. They would change the dressings on the burns and irrigate my bowel. During those ten-minute sessions I'd scream out like a child. In my desperation I'd grab hold of the cold metal headboard, close my eyes, and cry out, "God! Take away this pain!" It was the only prayer I could muster, and it never did any good. Or so I thought.

The whole scenario nearly sickened the nurses, especially after the gangrene set in. I later learned they drew straws to see who would get stuck with the gruesome chore.

And death lingered near. I overhead ominous whispers: "if he survives," and the even more frightening phrase, "as a vegetable." I knew the nurses were worried, so I wasn't surprised one day, about a week after the shooting, when a middle-aged man stood by my bed. He and I were alone in the room.

"Peter," the stranger said, calling me by name, "God did not give you this pain, nor will He take it away. But perhaps if you would pray for God to give you the strength to bear the pain, you might experience some relief."

He didn't stay long. I don't think he actually prayed with me. And I'm sure he didn't reach out and touch me. When he said what he needed to say, he left.

Many details are not clear. Was he wearing a green gown? I'm not sure. A clerical collar? Probably not. Did he *tell* me, or did I just sense that he was a minister recruited by one of the nurses to bring me comfort? One way or the other, I knew his vocation and that he'd been summoned for that purpose.

Soon after his visit, it was time for my next dreaded treatment. If the nurse had sent this minister in, I figured, it couldn't hurt to try his prescribed method. So I did.

As the gloved nurse fiddled with her utensils, I grabbed the headboard, closed my eyes, and prayed with my whole heart, "God, *please*, give me strength to bear this pain."

I waited a few long minutes. Having little faith I expected the pain to blast through my body. Finally I said to the nurse, "What are you waiting for? Is there a problem?"

She looked surprised. "I'm all through," she said. "You did real well this time."

All through? I hadn't felt a twinge when she'd torn off bandages or touched my wounds or flushed my system.

Nor did I ever again. From that day on, the doctors and nurses talked a new line: "recovery," even "miraculous healing."

The fever receded, allowing the surgeons to cut out the gangrene. The burns and wounds healed.

What's more, from that day to this, I've wanted to live. "Get rid of the guns," I told my wife when she visited one day. "I don't want them in the house."

I was in the hospital for a month, and about a month after my release, I returned to the hospital for an express purpose: to get the name of the minister the nurses had called in. I asked one, then another, and another.

They all remembered me well, and they all had the same story. "We didn't call anybody." The big, gruff head nurse joined the discussion: "Peter, we didn't recruit a minister. And you were under such heavy guard that no stranger got into your room. Your story doesn't add up. Maybe it was one of your hallucinations."

No. I stood my ground, and for one clear reason: Hallucinations don't heal. And I had been healed in body and in spirit.

Convalescing that summer, I learned to pray and meditate. As I listened to the Lord's words of life, I knew that my guardian angel had visited me. I may have prayed the wrong prayer, but God had been faithful in sending His healing message, that I should pray for *spiritual* commodities, which God could supply—and did supply, when I humbly opened my heart and asked Him. As I was willing to make a change in myself, God was eager to bless me beyond my imagination. And His spiritual healing ushered in a physical cure.

During that summer of treatment and recovery, doctors established that some unidentified brain abnormality, not a tumor, was causing my seizures. I remained under medication until 1967, when surgeons removed the culprit, a congenital cerebral aneurysm.

In my spirit I continued to grow, but ever so slowly and maybe like a perennial garden flower, dormant for a season and then shooting up with new evidence of life. My relationship with God was personal and private, disconnected from a body of believers who worshiped and prayed together.

The next ten years were not easy. My wife and I divorced. Although my son and I did not see each other daily, we remained close. From that tragic day when he as a toddler had crawled up the steps calling out for me, our bond has continued to grow.

In 1981 I remarried, and my new life set me in the midst of new challenges. My dear Martha suffered from a mental illness, paranoid-schizophrenia and manic-depression. When she was feeling well, life was wonderful. But then a winter season would descend on her spirit and she saw no hope of spring.

And yet Martha was a woman with a deep underlying faith. She quickly drew me into her church community, where I thrived on activity. Within a few years I was chairman of the men's group, a trained lay counselor in Stephen Ministries, and finally a member of the church board, the vestry.

Back home, night after night, Martha and I would join hands and pray together—for our well-being and fervently for Martha's healing. "Lord, take this illness away. Deliver Martha from this burden."

But once again, I must admit, the prayer seemed to have little effect. Martha's overall condition didn't seem to improve. If anything she grew worse, increasingly withdrawn, depressed, overcome with a restless darkness that sapped the joy from her spirit.

And once again, the Lord saw fit to nudge me to make a change in my spirit before He answered my prayer. This time the message came not by a stranger or angel, but by a word straight to my spirit, as I took part in a Sunday service early in the Epiphany season, 1992. In an Episcopal service, the congregation is given an opportunity to ask for prayers of intercession, especially for the sick. And as I quietly spoke Martha's name, requesting God's grace, I heard God's response: "Go home to Martha."

Go home to Martha. I knew what it meant. I was to give up much of the "activity" that kept me away from home evenings and weekends. I was to spend more time with my wife, easing her isolation, drawing her back into the world that on good days brought her so much joy.

The message was reminiscent of the minister's word in the hospital after my gunshot wound: Change your perspective. Open your heart. Pray a new prayer.

Again God gave me the grace to hear and to act on what I heard. Immediately I talked to the pastor, who suggested I take a temporary leave from some of my responsibilities. I took his advice, and, at the end of Epiphany, when I still felt as strongly about my call, I resigned.

Over the next eighteen months, I gave Martha my full attention. And in that care—as I changed—Martha blossomed, her illness receding, her smile returning.

For his own good reasons, God chose to take my Martha home to Him suddenly in November 1993, by a brain tumor that had no connection with her illness. The night before she died, I sat beside her bed at home, as she had requested. My hand on her pain ravished and burning head, I prayed that Martha would have strength to bear the pain *or* that God would take her to be home with Him, if that was His good will.

After my amen, she turned to me and said, "It's going to be okay, Peter. I have this peace—what Saint Paul described—the peace that passeth all understanding."

I felt that Martha's pain, even her spirit, left her body that night, though her breath held on until morning, until after the nurse had bathed her, changed her gown, and combed her hair. Martha never went anywhere without dressing properly.

One year later, though still grieving my loss and also facing a forced early retirement, I also knew that indescribable peace. Instead of panicking and feeling invalid, as so many retirees do and as I had felt as a young man facing an uncertain future, I felt a new freedom and anticipation. What was God's next step for me? I wasn't sure but I started each day with the words of prophet Isaiah: "Here I am, Lord, send me."

> *May the Lord give strength to his people!*
> *May the Lord bless his people with peace!*
> —Psalm 29:11 (RSV)

~ Melanie Emory ~

WHEN YOU FIRST MEET MELANIE EMORY it is 1989 and her name is Melanie
Fowler. She is a junior in high school. She is pretty, bright, innocent, and
experiencing the bewildering emotional stirrings that come on the cusp of
maturity. What you must know about Melanie, if you are to comprehend her
story fully, is that she lives a life dedicated to the Lord. Indeed, most of the
people she holds dear are similarly close to God. This is not unusual in the
rural territory you are about to visit, an area of camp meetings and revivalism
where the air is charged with spiritual voltage.

   Melanie has always lived in that westernmost part of North Carolina
squeezed between the Blue Ridge Mountains and the Great Smokies. Her
home is in Mills River, a town of one grocery store and a restaurant. Her
father, David Fowler, is a paramedic based in Hendersonville, ten miles away.

Melanie is an only child, which might be one reason why she and her mother, Kay, have always been such intimate friends. Kay is her daughter's confidante, so much so that Kay could have written this story herself; she keeps a daily journal in which most of the things you will read here are recorded just as Melanie told them to her at the time they happened.

The Fowler family worships at Words of Life Tabernacle in nearby Arden. The Reverend Paul Ramsey, a popular evangelist who travels widely through-out the South, often preaches there. Occasionally Melanie plays the piano at the Tabernacle services, a talent she perfected on her own, without any lessons, on a piano her grandmother purchased for fifty dollars.

Melanie was the Tabernacle pianist on the night when, "in the spirit," Reverend Ramsey saw "a vision of an angel with hands outstretched" standing behind Melanie. Her angel was not the only vision that the evangelist can tell you about seeing for there have been others. That no one else in the congregation saw the young woman's angelic vision he understands. He likens it to the vision found in the tenth chapter of Daniel when God sent a "certain man clothed in linen, whose loins were girded with fine gold of Uphaz… And I Daniel alone saw the vision: for the men that were with me saw not the vision… (Daniel 10:5-7, KJV).

Now, turn the pages of the calendar. It is five years later and Melanie is now Mrs. Philip Emory. The couple live in a house next door to Philip's parents beneath the Blue Ridge Parkway in Barnardsville, a place not any larger than Mills River. Philip is an electrician by trade, and, at the age of twenty-five, he has received his license to preach. More and more Philip and Melanie are venturing out on Sundays to different churches in the area. They are a team. He preaches and she provides the piano. Sometimes she will sing, sometimes a song that she herself has composed, just another example of the strange and wonderful part that music plays, and has played, in this young couple's lives—heavenly music.

90

In Good Hands

by Melanie Emory

And may the Lord hold you in the hollow of His hand.

—An Old Gaelic Blessing

THE SUMMER I WAS SEVENTEEN, I was miserable. Since grammar school, I had been the sweetheart of one particular boy. And now he wanted to marry me.

But when it came to marriage, I knew he wasn't the one for me. On one level the issue seemed spiritual: I had this deep inner feeling that this marriage wasn't part of God's plan. It was time to break off the relationship. Actually, I'd tried several times before, but my boyfriend always tugged me back.

I needed courage to try to say good-bye again—courage I couldn't seem to find in the hollow that nestles my hometown of Mills River, North Carolina.

My mother knew I wasn't happy. Sometimes I would wake in the middle of the night. Through the heat duct in my bedroom floor I could hear Mama downstairs in the den. She was begging God to hold me in the hollow of His hand.

Maybe her prayers set God's messenger in motion. Maybe they pushed me out of the house to camp meeting one night when I felt so sick.

Camp meeting is the highlight of the summer in our neighboring community of Arden. On a predetermined Friday, the men of Words of Life Tabernacle drag out the old orange and white circus tent. In the field in front of the church, they secure the poles and raise the roof. They spread sawdust over the mowed weeds and align rows of folding chairs. Once you see the big box of hot-weather fans—cardboard stapled to paint stirrers—you know it's time for revival to roll down from heaven.

As a teenager I was always one of the first ones there. That's because I was one of the piano players, even though I'd never had a music lesson. When I was five my grandmother had bought me an old upright piano, which became my favorite toy. I tell people the Lord taught me how to play, hymns and gospel songs.

I loved camp meeting. But one midweek night I told my mother I just couldn't go. My head hurt. My body ached. "I'm coming down with something," I said. Besides my physical complaints, it was as if the mountains around the Mills River hollow were closing in and suffocating my spirit. I was depressed. Fearful. Confused about my future.

But at the last minute, I changed my mind and my clothes. I pulled on a despised yellow skirt, because everything else I owned needed to be ironed. I brushed my hair into a ponytail, because I didn't have time to curl it. I didn't really care how I looked, because something inside told me that my whole future depended on my getting inside the revival tent.

Early in the service I accompanied the congregation as it sang a Southern favorite, "Amazing Grace." And that's what hit me near the end of the sermon, based on Ephesians 1:10-12 (NKJV), which refers to the purposes of God "who works all things according to the counsel of His will." The preacher, the Reverend Paul Ramsey, a traveling evangelist who made his home in our valley, kept returning to one point: the love and good purpose of God Who knew us before we were conceived. "God wants you to trust Him with your life."

About halfway through the sermon, I suddenly felt as if every hair on my body was standing on end, reaching for the sky. I'd recently read an article about people who'd survived lightning strikes. They'd talked about the goose bumps and raised hair that immediately preceded the blow.

I'm not going to be hit by lightning, am I? With that thought I looked up toward the peak of the tent and saw a ball of light coming through the canvas. It was bright like the sun, about the size of a basketball. At first it hovered near the top of the center pole. Then it darted downward toward me. I froze, waiting for the lightning to strike, but it never hit. It simply disappeared.

I looked around to see how everyone else was reacting to the extraordinary phenomenon. But the service hadn't been interrupted. Rev. Ramsey hadn't lost his stride. Mama was still waving her cardboard fan. No one looked puzzled or petrified.

I've got to get to the altar, I thought. *I don't know what I'll pray, but I've got to talk to God. I'm here tonight for some reason. I've got to find out what this is about.*

At the end of the sermon, I didn't worry about getting to the piano bench for the last song. I bolted down the sawdust aisle to the altar. I didn't want to hold back the tears, and I silently cried out to God: *If You'll give me strength to do what I need to do, I'll serve You the rest of my life.*

While Rev. Ramsey invited others to come forward, I sensed someone standing behind me. I quickly glanced over my shoulder to see which deacon had come to pray with me. But no one was there. Suddenly, Rev. Ramsey stopped talking. He walked over to me. I opened my closed eyes and saw his black dress shoes. When he spoke his voice quavered: "People, can you see what I see? The angel of the Lord is standing behind this young lady. Its arms are stretched out over her."

My body started to quake. I sobbed uncontrollably. The goose bumps returned—that same feeling I'd had with the ball of light. It was as if the hairs on my arms were being attracted by an awesome love that wafted over me. The congregation, usually full of amen-ers, was stone silent. I didn't turn around. Whatever was there was too awesome to see.

Rev. Ramsey spoke directly to me. "Melanie, the Lord's angels are going to minister to you throughout the night."

After the dismissal I didn't linger at the altar. God had something *more* for me. I had to get home and find out what it was.

After the service my boyfriend drove me home. "What's happening, Melanie?" he asked. "I didn't see an angel—and your mother didn't—but the preacher did. And you—what's wrong?" I was still shaky, not myself.

"I just can't talk now," I tried to explain. "And please don't talk to me. This is important. I need to get to my bedroom to see what the preacher was talking about."

"But we always go to the Dairy Queen after service. Melanie—"

"Just take me home, please. God's not finished and I don't want to mess this up."

When he pulled up in front of my house, I jumped out and ran in, past my father in the living room, straight to my room. I quickly dressed for bed and settled between the sheets. I turned out the table lamp. Alone in the dark I raised my hands toward the ceiling, praising God, asking for more of His touch. Crying again, tears of joy, I glanced toward the open window across the room. At that instant five bright balls of light swept in through the screen. Each was as bright as the light I'd seen in the tent, but much smaller, the size of a bumblebee. Like five lively fireflies, they flew in a random pattern about two feet above my head.

The longer they stayed, the more of an awesome presence I felt. The preacher had said that angels would minister to me all night. These fireflies were angels—I was sure they were.

The small lights were still glowing when I finally fell asleep. When I woke in the morning, they were gone. They left no visible sign of their visit. But in the night they'd filled my spirit full of a courage I thought I'd never find in Mills River.

I used that courage to tell my boyfriend once and for all that we weren't meant for each other. I told him about the fireball and the fireflies. And he'd seen for himself the intensity in Rev. Ramsey's eyes. "I've tried to tell you before, but this time I'm sure. We shouldn't get married. It's not what God wants for us. That's the message the angels left in my spirit."

He sat very quietly. This time he understood and didn't try to convince me to change my mind.

I tie the amazing life-changing events that happened later that autumn to that camp-meeting night and the courage-bearing angels. You see, to allow my old boyfriend and me some breathing room, my dad suggested that our family visit other churches for a while. So one Sunday morning in September, Mama wanted to go to the church of a friend of hers, the Church of God in Woodfin, about twenty miles away.

I'd never been in this church before. As we walked in late, during a congregational song, I glanced around the large sanctuary. An impressive wooden cross hung on the wall behind the pulpit. And an impressive young man stood in the back row of the choir. I couldn't get my eyes off him…his broad smile, blue eyes, dark curly hair. During the sermon I had to force myself to concentrate on the message and not on the tenor wearing the red tie. *God, forgive me for being so distracted*, I prayed. *And help me pay attention.*

It's as if the preacher himself heard my prayer. In the middle of his message, he abruptly interrupted himself. Suddenly, he had *everyone's* attention: "This is very unusual for me. But the Lord is telling me to say that there are two people in this congregation whose destiny will be fulfilled this day."

Like the ball of fire in the revival tent, the words darted to my spirit. I nudged my mother's arm. "Mama, he's talking to me."

She raised her eyebrows, acknowledging what I said but also telling me to *hush*.

O Lord, what's this about? I wondered. *Whatever it means, I'm ready.*

After the service, before we even got out into the aisle, that young smiling man walked up to me. He looked right into my eyes as he reached to shake my hand. "Hello. I'm Philip Emory," he said.

I introduced myself and my mother, and Philip asked if we'd be able to come back for the evening service.

At six we were there, and Philip greeted us again after the service. "I know you're going to think I'm very forward, but I'd like to take you and your mother out to dinner." Nothing fancy—the Pizza Hut in Asheville.

Mama smiled at me and then at him. Yes, she said, we'd be delighted. At the restaurant I picked at one piece of pizza. I still couldn't keep my eyes off this young man. This just wasn't like me. And Mama was acting out of character also. There was always a mother-hen quality about her; she was very particular about whom I was out with. But this night she agreed that Philip and I could take our time and that he could drive me home to Mills River. "I can go on ahead. You two can stay awhile."

As I toyed with that pizza, I admitted my excitement about the day. "I think it was destiny that I came to Woodfin this morning."

Philip wasn't subtle in his reply: "Well, you know it is. Didn't you hear the preacher?"

As we talked Philip fiddled with a straw wrapper. Before we left he slid his handiwork across the table to me: He'd twisted it in the shape of a ring. "Melanie, I think we've got something here."

When he delivered me back home, I met Mama in the living room. When we were alone I started to cry. I remember her response. "Well, young lady, you just might be Mrs. Emory one day." Was this my mother speaking? The woman I thought wanted me to live with her until I died?

I walked to my room thinking, *This must be the Lord.*

In the next month, I saw a lot of Philip. He was only nineteen, but he had a seasoned gift for preaching. An electrician by trade, he felt a call to be an evangelist.

Was it a coincidence that for years I'd felt that I would someday marry a preacher?

Was it a coincidence that he'd been praying for a wife who was a musician?

In the pulpit his words came as naturally to him as my music came to me. Was it a coincidence that we'd both been "taught by God"?

Lord, I prayed, *can it be? Can this be the future You have for me?*

God chose to send me another answer directly from the heavens. On a seventy-degree Sunday that October, Philip and I went for a drive along the colorful Blue Ridge Parkway. "Let's drive up along the river," I suggested, wanting to show Philip some countryside he'd never seen before.

In no hurry to get to the parkway, we stopped to enjoy the view at the old Baptist Church along Mills River. The white frame building deserves a page on a "Come to Carolina" calendar. Secluded from neighbors, hidden against the sycamore trees, its high steeple holds a silver bell that reigns over the landscape; a well-kept yard spreads down to the riverbank and surrounding woods.

There was an old homemade quilt in the car, and we spread it out over the grass near the river. After a while, our talk turned sentimental, prompting Philip to say, "Let's pray about our future and God's will." Holding hands, on our knees facing each other, we talked to God, Philip aloud and I in my spirit. I listened as Philip placed our future in God's hands. He said he wanted to serve God; he was willing to preach, even if it meant leaving the security of his trade as an electrician. "And, Father, I thank you for giving me this helpmeet."

There was no doubt in my mind that Philip and I were someday to become one, and minister the Gospel of Jesus Christ together.

Philip kept praying but suddenly I was distracted. In the distance I began to hear music, beautiful music. It grew louder and louder. I looked at Philip. He had a startled look on his face. We were hearing the same music—and we were awed. The music soared and then voices, heavenly voices singing praises and blessings. Philip and I had tears in our eyes. The sound receded until finally, after maybe ten minutes, it faded out of our range. All we could hear was the rumble of the river and the mockingbirds in the woods.

In the quiet Philip took my hand. "God's given us a sign of His blessing," Philip said with great surety.

Philip and I waited three years before we married, on September 12, 1992, in a quaint wedding chapel in Gatlinburg, Tennessee. As I said my "I do," my thoughts went out to the heavenly choir that had blessed my future with this chosen man.

After the reception we drove to our honeymoon hideaway, a nearby mountain chalet. That evening we snuggled in front of a fireplace fire. As we nibbled on party food my mother had packed up for us, our conversation turned to how God's purpose for our lives could now begin. And so it did.

As we marked our second anniversary, Philip and I restored and moved into the original homeplace that his grandfather had built. It's not in Mills River but in Philip's hometown, in another hollow, just a few houses nestled in a dip between North Carolina hills.

Every morning I wake and look up across the wooded slopes. Those hills remind me that our future rests secure in the hollow of His hand.

Angel voices, ever singing
Round thy throne of light,
Angel harps forever ringing,
Rest not day nor night;
Thousands only live to bless thee,
And confess thee, Lord of might.

Thou, who art beyond the farthest
Mortal eye can scan,
Can it be that Thou regardest
Sons of sinful man?
Can we feel that Thou art near us
And wilt hear us? Yea, we can.

Here, great God, today we offer
Of Thine own to Thee;
And for Thine acceptance proffer
All unworthily,
Hearts and minds, and hands and voices,
In our choicest melody.

—Author Unknown

Fay Angus

THERE ARE MANY MESSENGERS in the story that Fay Angus has to tell. The one you will most remember—and Fay cannot forget— is a mysterious man in a raincoat who spoke to her in terms that were anything but obscure: "Don't be afraid. Remember you are never alone. God is always with you."

This was not the mysterious man's only message, but it was the one that Fay did not have to ponder. She had known about God's protective love since her childhood days in a Catholic convent school in Shanghai, China. "I owe that security," she says, "to the sweetness of the nuns there who gave me the assurance that I was not alone. I was one of those fortunate children who was never afraid of the dark." Later, as a teenager, this fearlessness stood her in good stead during the two and a half years she and her mother were held captive in a Japanese prison camp at Yangchow during World War II.

Obviously, Fay is a woman with an unusual history. Her mother and father were both born in China. Her paternal, Australian grandfather was a missionary at Kien Ping, and her maternal, English grandfather was the commander of a large British garrison that trained Chinese army officers in an isolated post in China's interior. Fay, however, was born in Brisbane, Australia, where her grandparents were then in retirement. Fay's mother used to love to say—with some truth—that her daughter was "born in a kangaroo's pocket and has been on the hop ever since." Australia, China, British Columbia, the United States—all of these places have been home for her, and though she and her civil engineer husband John have lived for nearly forty years in Sierra Madre, California, Fay persists in thinking of Shanghai as her hometown!

Fay is a writer. She has published—at last count—twelve books. A simple listing of their titles would give you a fair description of this cheerful, caring, many-sided woman. Her books range from *The White Pagoda*, the story of her youth in China; to *The Gentle Art of Being There*, a paean to friendship; to *How to Do Everything Right and Live to Regret It* (with an impish smile she'll say she's about to write a sequel called *How to Do Everything Wrong and Thoroughly Enjoy It*—don't believe her).

A regular contributor to the annual *Daily Guideposts* devotional, Fay is currently deep into her first novel, a very serious, often grim narrative based on her father's efforts to survive his capture when Hong Kong fell to the enemy in the 1940s. She is often away on speaking engagements, frequently at women's spiritual conferences. "It's pretty much my schedule," Fay reports, "that I write during the week and run to the airport on the weekend."

It's surprising that Fay has not written a book about angels; she believes implicitly in their existence ("I always see them as men"), and she has had more than one adventure in which her "defending angel," as she calls him, appeared.

But for now, Fay has a mysterious man in a raincoat she wants you to meet....

Be at My Side to Rule and Guide

by Fay Angus

O Lord, you know what is best for me. Let this or that be done, as you please. Give what you will, how much you will, and when you will.

—Thomas à Kempis

THE SISTERS AT SHANGHAI'S CONVENT of the Sacred Heart taught their students well. Reading, writing, arithmetic, and habits of the heart. As a six-year-old, first-grade student I memorized a prayer that I repeated once a day by rote:

> *Angel of God, my guardian dear,*
> *to whom His love commits me here.*
> *Ever this day be at my side,*
> *to light and guard, to rule and guide.*

But by the time I was nine, I wasn't sure my prayers counted for anything. It was the day Mother Gabrielle drew me aside, into a private corner of the recreation room; she pulled the drapes to give us privacy; she sat next to me and put one hand tenderly on my head.

"*Ma chère petite* Fay," she began. Then she quietly told me that my brother Maurice had died. "He has gone to be with Jesus." I burst into tears, and she steadied my head against her shoulder. Maurice's appendix had burst, she explained. Surgery. Sickness. Death. "He is with Jesus, little Fay," she repeated.

After prayers in the chapel, I asked to go out into the garden and be alone. And there I talked to heaven: "I don't want him with Jesus. I want him here with ME!" I rubbed my fingers along the granite grotto until they bled.

By age fifteen, I still had questions of God and his ways. After the Japanese invasion of China, my mother and I, along with six hundred other Westerners, had been sent on a slow, miserable boat to Yangchow Internment Camp C. Let's just say I grew up fast, knowing hunger and cold and fear.

On the whole our captors left us alone, provided we obeyed all the regulations and roll calls. But a couple of commandants were more aggressive, hauling us out of bed in the middle of the night for a count, expecting us to stand interminably in the snow with cracked, chilblained feet poking out through hole-worn shoes.

But God had not deserted that camp. He sent this young discouraged, and confused teenager a series of messengers that led to a vital relationship with Him. The first was a missionary willing to teach history in our make-shift school; after classes he taught a Bible study that introduced me to a Book I knew about but had never actually read.

Another was a seventeen-year-old missionary's son named Dobbs who carried a big black Bible—and helped me with my math lessons. Studying together one day, we noticed a third messenger: *the guard*, walking back and forth on top of a nearby wall. I don't know, maybe he'd noticed that huge Bible Dobbs carried. Whatever the reason, the guard started singing in Japanese to the tune of "Onward Christian Soldiers." As his confidence grew, he sang louder and louder until he reached a triumphant crescendo, and then he stopped, just as suddenly as he had begun and continued his slow, silent pacing.

"Do you think he's a Christian?" I asked Dobbs.

"I don't know. Maybe he went to a missionary school in Japan. Maybe he just heard the tune from a church and put his own Japanese words to it."

"Maybe he's trying to tell us something! Maybe he's trying to encourage us!"

Dobbs had the final word: "He's a sign from God that we're going to be all right."

A fourth messenger brought me to a personal relationship with God. A pig-tailed school chum handed me her most precious possession—her own Bible, inscribed in perfect print: "To Fay, from Carol. Camp C Yangchow—31st of May 1945."

That gift was a turning point for me, and one week past my sixteenth birthday, the hand of the Almighty reached down to claim me as His own. Having seen such evidence of His love, I gave Him my heart and asked Him to be my rule and my guide.

After the war Mother and I floundered—until she agreed to accept her brother's invitation to make a new life with him, in British Columbia, Canada.

As we sailed through the Straits of Georgia under the famous Lion's Gate Bridge, my heart raced with excitement. Vancouver! Its waterfront skyline promised the fulfillment of my youthful dreams. I was just seventeen. I would sit for my college entrance exams, enroll in the University of British Columbia, and pursue a teaching career.

But Vancouver proved to be full of surprises. Instead of the warm home fires we expected at Uncle Bill's, we walked into a blazing divorce controversy. "You should have written and told us.... We never would have come.... Whatever can we do?"

Equally endeared to both my aunt and uncle, we were caught in the crossfire of a domestic war.

My mother's health, already fragile from the captivity and privation, steadily declined. Pernicious anemia. Acute anxiety. High blood pressure. At her prime, at age forty-seven, Mother felt life slipping out from under her.

After seven or eight months of buffeting our way through unresolved family conflicts, we moved to one of the many walk-up apartments in Vancouver's West End. On the second floor we shared one all-purpose room with a closet-turned-kitchen. We shared a bath with the woman next door.

Feeling utterly lost in this new world, we both spent long hours on a bench under the willows that rimmed the path around Lost Lagoon in Stanley Park. In those months I let go of my dream of a teaching career. To make ends meet, I took a part-time job as a junior clerk in an accounting office. To improve my skills, I enrolled in a secretarial course two nights a week.

When she was well enough, Mother often worked in Uncle Bill's antique store, just around the corner from the famous Hudson Bay Company, an ideal location to draw in the serious shopper or casual passerby. The shelves of Uncle Bill's shop were lined with the porcelain, Dynasty vases, jades, and other fine art he'd brought from China before the war.

One gray, drizzly afternoon late in 1947, Mother walked into the apartment, having spent the day at the store. From the makeshift kitchen, where I was making a sandwich to eat on the trolley going across town to my evening class, I looked up and saw her red-rimmed eyes. Once again she was on the brink of tears, which came too easily to her these days, and I was worried. "Could you please skip your class and stay home tonight? I'm going to need you to be here with me." Her voice trembled.

"Mother, what's wrong?"

She poured out a strange story: "Right after the mailman left the store, I started sobbing. I just couldn't bear it anymore. I even pounded my fists on the desk in the back of the store and cried out loud, 'I hate it here!' Suddenly, I heard this gentle voice right behind me. 'My dear woman, why do you hate it here?'

"I turned around and saw a man standing in front of the display case. He was about my age and he wore a raincoat, a dry raincoat, though it was raining outside. I was shocked. I don't know where he came from. I'm sure I would have heard him if he'd come in the door. I always do.

"I was embarrassed that I hadn't been attentive. I apologized, 'I'm sorry. I didn't see you come in.'

"'No matter,' he said and then he bluntly asked, 'Why are you so unhappy?' Like a gentleman he took my elbow and gently set me into that carved teak chair behind the desk.

"I can't believe it—it's not like me, you know—but I sat there and sobbed out my story...my health, Bill's troubles, our future...your future—this is no life for you, Fay....

"He was a stranger. How could I possibly have blurted out all this to a perfect stranger?

"Well, then, customers walked in. Of course I had to pull myself together and wait on them. As I got up, this man leaned over and said, 'I will come and see you tonight.' Then he was gone. Not through the front door, not through the curtain to the back door. He just disappeared."

"Did you give him your address?" I asked.

"No. I didn't even give him my name. He just said he would come."

I threw up my hands. "All this is beyond me. But if it makes you feel better, I'll skip my class and stay home."

We ate sandwiches for dinner. As we sipped our tea, we could hear the rain pelting outside the window. That's when the doorbell rang.

My mother gulped. "Do you think?"

I sprang to the door, turned the knob, and gasped. *Oh, my! It's the man, no question*—exactly as Mother had described him. Middle-aged. Graying at the temples. A bone-dry, London Fog-type raincoat. *The mystery stranger. How did he find us? What does he want?*

My eyes locked onto his, and I smiled. "How do you do?" I asked, reaching to shake his hand. "I'm afraid I don't know your name."

His smile radiated peace. "No matter," he answered. From his firm handclasp, a tingling warmth moved up my arm, prompting me to draw him fearlessly into our home. We offered him a cup of tea, but he refused, saying he could stay just a short while.

Though his earlier visit had been to comfort Mother, this evening he seemed to want to talk about me. Pulling up a chair, he sat and looked straight into my eyes. "You will find your dream," he said. "There is purpose in your being here."

Then he spoke to both of us: "Don't be afraid. Remember you are never alone. God is always with you. Whenever you are feeling sad, pray. I will know you are praying, and I will be praying with you."

He didn't stay more than five minutes. As he rose to leave, he put his large hand on my head, crushing down my curls as though to leave an imprint. "You are blessed," he said intently.

Then his hand went to my mother's head, his fingers spread slightly apart so that the tips curved down to press against her forehead. "You are blessed," he repeated.

Without a further word, he opened the door and let himself out. As he shut the door behind him, I turned to Mother. "We never asked how he found us," I whispered.

"No matter," she replied with a quaint smile. She paused. We stared at each other, our minds racing, trying to fathom what had just happened. Then Mother said the words: "He was an angel."

Yes, I knew he was.

A mantle of peace fell over Mother and me; with it came the assurance that we were being looked after, cared for.

As I fell asleep that night I found myself whispering, "Angel of God, my guardian dear," the sweet prayer of my childhood. And now all doubts fell away; I prayed with complete conviction. I knew I had an angel with me…"to light and guard, to rule and guide." I claimed the angel promise, "You are blessed, Fay. You are blessed."

I never did get to college. God's vision for my future was much bigger than my own. Within a few short weeks of our angel visitor, at eleven-thirty one night, the doorbell rang persistently. *Buzzz, buzzz.*

For heaven's sake, I thought as I pulled on a kimono, *get your finger off it. I'm coming.* I threw open the door and collided at eye level with a red and black Pendleton shirt. A pair of heavy logger's boots came within inches of treading on my bare toes. In a sleepy daze, I looked up. Paul Bunyan himself! A tall, husky man towered above me.

He rubbed his fingers through a head full of platinum curls and peered down at me through heavy-rimmed glasses. "Say, I'm sorry!" he apologized. "I'm John Angus. I'm just down from a logging stint up at Port Alberni. I thought this was my sister Jean's apartment."

Jean lived next door. Beautiful and talented, she sang light opera with Vancouver's popular Theatre under the Stars in Stanley Park.

"That's Jean's apartment, down the hall," I explained, "but she has a performance tonight. Would you care to come in for a cup of tea and wait for her here?"

"Thanks." He stepped inside and clunked his duffel bag down onto the floor.

As he pulled up a chair (the same "angel" chair), I looked him over. *A curious man. Rugged. Different. Interesting.* I liked his name, John Angus. Made me think of swirling kilts bobbing to the pitch of bagpipes.

In a twinkling, as though God suddenly snapped His fingers, I stepped into the beginning of many dreams come true! That night John and I found each other. First in friendship, then in a romance that led to the glorious blessing of marriage, our move to the hills of Southern California and the joy of raising a family.

When the children were in school, a dormant dream surfaced. I started to write. Little did I know that far beyond my own limited vision, almighty God was training me to share the experiences of my life by the written word and on the speaker's platform.

When my first book was published, I held it in my hands, the tears of joy streaming down my face. I turned to John and said, "Can you believe, honey? A dream come true…and I didn't even get to college!"

Several published books later, I was asked to speak at a writers' day at a local city college. "But I don't have a college degree," I stammered. It didn't matter; they liked my work.

Teaching! I was terrified. I remembered the angel's words, "You will find your dream! Pray. I will know you are praying, and I will be praying with you."

As I took the podium and faced an auditorium of several hundred bright young students, I prayed. I can still feel the relief of the applause after that first presentation. And the joy of answering students' questions and encouraging those who were discouraged and ready to give up to "keep on writing!"

"Yes," I whispered, as to my angel friend, "I am most truly blessed."

I could fill this whole book with scenes of God's blessing, days when I rejoiced over His grace in my life. One of the most significant was in 1989, when I flew to London for a reunion with some four hundred ex-POWs from China.

Carol, who had given me her Bible in the prison camp, was there, minus her pigtails. I hadn't see her for more than forty years. We hugged each other as if we never wanted to let go. Carol sat with me at the special service of thanksgiving in the historic royal chapel in Windsor Castle (since then tragically gutted by fire).

We all sang together that wonderful Isaac Watts hymn:

> *O God our help in ages past,*
> *Our hope for years to come,*
> *Be thou our guide while life shall last,*
> *And our eternal home.*

As the refrain echoed off the massive stone walls, it was as if my life had suddenly come full circle. I once again felt that angel touch upon my head— the blessing of survival through devastating hardship, the blessing of many new beginnings, the blessing of friendship, and the overwhelming blessing of God's presence.

Now facing my senior years, I could see the fulfillment of the angel's message to me as a discouraged young woman groping my way toward an uncertain future. *You are never alone. God is always with you. You are blessed.*

My daughter, Katrelya, in her early thirties, is now reaching out through uncertainty toward dreams. Unlike me, she went to college and has a degree in English lit. But the teaching career she envisioned stayed behind a closed door that didn't crack open. And the word processing business she is struggling to get launched is slow in taking off. Does she hear my motherly assurances that the Lord wants to bless all his children? I'm not always sure. But just last week, I stepped back and smiled, knowing I wasn't the only one giving her this message.

One Tuesday morning Katrelya ran in the house clutching a bright magenta plaster angel. Her eyes were wide with wonder, her face flushed with excitement.

"Mom, look!" she held out the figure. The angel was a cherub, in a sitting position, about eighteen inches high. An attached bright magenta banner attached said, "Look for angels."

"Where on earth did you get that?" I asked, taking the figure from her for a better look. It was heavy.

"I was jogging the trail up behind the house, when I just found this, sitting on the edge of the footbridge across the wash. Look, it's signed."

Sure enough. "Jill D'Agnecia—'94" was painted in black on the base of the figure. And it came with a small printed explanation: The angel was part of a contemporary art project, funded by the Rockefeller Foundation and the Andy Warhol Foundation, to place 4,687 magenta plaster angels around Los Angeles, the City and County "of Angels." I read further: Each angel was being prayerfully positioned by a team of volunteers. The project wanted to bring hope and healing after the devastation of earthquakes, fires, and riots that had recently caused such suffering to so many in our community.

"Do you think it's a sign from God, to encourage me?" Katrelya asked.

I smiled. Tears welling up in my eyes, I nodded yes.

My daughter, at a time of great need, had found the message and the blessing of an angel!

We hugged each other, and I placed my hand on her head as we quietly said together the angel prayer I had learned as a child and had passed along to her throughout her growing years:

> *Angel of God, my guardian dear,*
> *to whom His love commits me here.*
> *Ever this day be at my side,*
> *to light and guard, to rule and guide.*

114

PART THREE

Angels Watching... In the Afternoon

O Lord, revive Your work

   in the midst of the years!

In the midst of the years

   make it known

In wrath, remember mercy.

     —Habakkuk 3:2 (NKJV)

～ Linda Johnston ～

DRAWING AND PAINTING have always been Linda Johnston's special talents, as well as her favorite pastime. In the beginning she liked to do landscapes, particularly her Grandpa Swyers' farm outside Rolla, Missouri, where she had a hundred acres of happy childhood memories to draw upon—cows and wheat fields and the big barn she used to play in. Drop in on Linda today at her home outside of Jackson, Mississippi, and you'll find that her subjects are now down to one: angels. And more specifically, a single angel, the one she has known most of her life, the one she has seen and talked to and whose soft voice she would recognize anywhere, anytime.

Recreating her angel on paper and canvas has been a major challenge. Linda has experimented in charcoal, oil and acrylic. She's even come up with a drawing created on a computer. She's talked extensively with her sister who knows sign language in an effort to better comprehend the delicate, fluid movements of her angel's hands. Again and again she has tried to capture the most elusive element of all, the light emanating from her angel, a rippling brightness, penetrating, yet not so intense that you would have to shield your eyes from its glare.

"My angel does not have wings," Linda says, "and yet most of the great artists of the past have painted them that way. I've often wondered if those old masters actually saw fluttering wings or whether that incredible shimmering light created an impression of thousands of quivering feathers."

For fourteen years Linda worked as a manager of fast food restaurants in the Jackson area, but her health won't permit that anymore. Her husband Herbie is a Texan whom she met while he was in high school. Retired now, until recently he was vice president of an environmental protection system company. They have two adolescent daughters, Marla and Sandra.

One of the things that is different about the Johnston home since the events of Linda's story is the Bible. "We used to keep it somewhere on a shelf in the back of the house," Linda says. "Now it's right here in my room in plain sight—where I can get at it."

And get at it she does. Constantly. And whenever she comes to a passage about angels, she takes out a yellow marker and flags it. She's getting to know the angels of the Bible almost as well as she knows her own angel. Almost, but not quite.

"It's Not Your Time"

by Linda Johnston

Angels, sing on! your faithful watches keeping;
Sing us sweet fragments of the songs above;
Till morning's joy shall end the night of weeping,
And life's long shadows break in cloudless love.

—Frederick W. Faber

HORTLY AFTER MY THIRTIETH BIRTHDAY, the mailman delivered a package from my mother who lives more than five hundred miles away in Springfield, Missouri. I let my young daughters Marla and Sandra rip off the wrapping. When I saw what was inside, I was as excited as they were.

It was an eight-by-ten copy of a small print that had hung on the wall of my bedroom, back in the fifties. In the painting a girl and boy are cowering on a bridge. They think they're lost and alone, but they're not. In the background an angel hovers near, present in the night.

I called and thanked my mother for the print.

"When I saw that, I just had to get it for you," she said.

"I'll hang it in the bedroom, Mom. Right next to my bed."

Every Mississippi morning I awoke strengthened by that artist's silent message. And strength I needed: as manager of a fast-food restaurant; as volunteer extraordinaire, always saying yes to anyone's plea for help; as a wife and mother who was "there," eager to go hiking or hunting with my family.

I've always been energized by being in—and painting—the great outdoors. In grammar school, inspired by this angel painting and other art, I took an interest in drawing. Pictures, I discovered, described a scene better than words. With pencil and paints I worked to re-create the world I loved, out-doors in the country on or near my grandparents' farm: the apple trees and fences I climbed; the rivers I rowed and waded in; the goldenrod fields where my grandfather and I watched the deer feed; the ponds and streams I fished, sometimes with Grandpa, sometimes alone.

Out in the wild I had time to think about angels. Not just what they looked like in pictures, but what they sounded like, because I'd heard them. At least I'd heard one of them for certain. The first time, I was fishing alone in one of Grandpa's three round farm-ponds when I heard someone call my name. "Linda?" I thought it was my grandmother calling from the back porch.

"I'm coming, just a minute," I hollered back. Then, at the house, "Yes, Grandma. What do you want?"

Grandma insisted she hadn't called me. The same thing happened again on another day, and the third or fourth time, Grandma said, "It must be the angels calling."

Angels? That was the first I knew that such a thing could really exist. They were there to watch over me, Grandma explained, and what a fortunate little girl I was to have heard them speak. Did Grandma know what she was talking about?

It seemed so. That's the only way I could explain a number of childhood days shrouded in mystery. Like the school morning in second grade when I walked several blocks and crossed a boulevard before boarding a Springfield city bus. My mother had taught me well. I looked both ways. And when I saw a clear street, I stepped out.

Screeeeech. I heard the high-pitched grinding of brakes just as I saw a car's front bumper. And instantly someone behind me grabbed my shirt collar and yanked me back to the sidewalk. I spun around to see who had pulled me out of the street. But no one was there. Someone had saved my life. But who?

Five years later my mother and I walked in the house from an afternoon of shopping, our arms full of groceries. Inside the kitchen door, we stopped and stared at each other. The house was full of the most beautiful, soothing choir music I'd ever heard. There were no actual words; many voices in perfect harmony sang music like a hymn. I could distinguish the soprano and alto singers. The basses joined in sometimes, then they'd drop out.

I set the groceries on the kitchen table and went into the living room, then through the bedrooms. Mom was right behind me. The TV was off. So was the radio. The hi-fi was still. No one else was in the house. Definitely, the sound was loudest in the living room.

"You hear it too?" I asked Mom.

"Yes, a big choir."

And then came the sound of a director's baton, hitting a music stand. It seemed as though we were hearing a rehearsal; the choir stopped and then began again, as if starting over—to get it right.

The music didn't last long, less than a minute. At the finale, the director said something like, "Okay, we'll go on now," as if it were time to practice a new number. Both Mom and I heard this, a whisper that faded away while he was still talking. Then we stood there. Just the two of us. In silence.

When I told my seventh-grade science teacher what had happened, he said it was probably some phenomenon of bouncing sound waves. I listened to him respectfully, but I knew something else was going on. My grandma had told me to listen for the angels.

Until I was thirty-eight years old, I had no clear explanation for these mysteries. But then on September 27, 1992, my world shattered. On the bridge between life and death, I had a conversation with my guardian angel.

It started with a seemingly inconsequential slip of the hand. Out in our garage-turned-art-studio, cutting a cardboard stencil for my husband's hunting gear, I gashed my left wrist, a deep gash almost four inches long. Pressing back the gushing blood, I yelled for my husband and headed for the kitchen. He found me there, hunched over the sink. "Herb, hurry, get me a towel. I've cut myself with that new roller-blade knife. It's going to need stitches."

Herb and the girls, sixteen and ten, gathered round. Herb called the emergency room at Methodist Hospital in Jackson, telling them to expect us in about twenty-five minutes. The girls begged to ride along. I think they were afraid of what might happen if they let their wounded mother out of their sight.

"No, no," I insisted. "It needs to be sewn up. But I haven't cut an artery. It's not serious. We'll be home in a couple of hours. You need to stay here and finish your homework."

I climbed into the front of our Toyota pickup that doubled as a camper. What you might call a nervous driver, I was always willing to let Herb drive. But tonight there was no question. I continued to press against my wrist and brace myself against the throbbing pain.

I hated pain. I didn't dwell on the prospects, but in the past when I'd seen or thought about the possibility of dying, I had breathed one prayer: "God, please don't let it hurt."

We were more than halfway to the hospital and were just crossing the overpass on Highway 18 when I felt a strange jolt. Herb cried out, "Hold on, Babe. We've been hit."

I prayed my short prayer: "Dear God, please don't let it hurt." I heard something like a shotgun blowing out a glass window. I heard the breath rush from my lungs and then...

I felt myself rising—as if I were standing in a Ferris wheel—far above the pavement, and going so fast I could feel the wind rushing by my face. Up. Up. Up. When I stopped, I sensed but couldn't see a floor and walls, as if I were in a very large room. Dark and peaceful, warm and soft, yet not a frightening enclosure. Though I didn't know where I was, I knew what had happened. Our truck had been hit hard from behind.

Where am I? What's going on? Oh, this is really weird. I can see colors and light and dark. I can smell flowers. I can hear music, yes, choir music. I can think. I can talk, but I am not talking. I am warm. I'm not afraid. But I don't know where I am.

I turned my head. To the left I saw only a dark blue hue that turned to black. To my right the blue was lighter, a cobalt blue so bright you'd think it would hurt your eyes, but its beauty captured my amazement.

For a second I turned back to the left, into the utter darkness. And then to the brighter right, where a shimmering angel floated down from above. I felt dwarfed in her presence. She could have cradled me in the crook of her arm as a mother holds a baby. Despite her size, her demeanor radiated a peace that, as the Bible says, passes beyond human understanding. Her hair was pulled back and covered by a blue shawl that fell down over her folded arms. Her long white gown blew as if there were a wind, though I felt none. Maybe it was the artist in me that started to analyze things, like the movement of her robe. *That's not a left-and-right or front-and-back wind. It's blowing from inside, going out in every direction.*

The light that broke into the darkness was alive and it came from the angel herself. It was like hundreds of small lights all coming from one spot but each with its own wavelength; it included rays of fluorescent blue and yellow. *Where is the light coming from?*

It's her heart, I soon figured. *It's as if the light breathes along with her.*

Finally she spoke. "You know me," she stated. The voice was calm, distinct, familiar.

I looked her up and down, "Yes," I said softly.

Though I'd never seen her before, I knew the voice, the feminine voice that had called my name as a child, fishing at my grandparents, swinging in my own backyard. I knew she'd grabbed my shirt collar and pulled me out of the street when I was in second grade. She'd been part of the choir singing in my Springfield living room. And she'd been silent at my side on thousands of nondescript days.

I heard her voice, but she also spoke with her hands, in a universal sign language I immediately understood. "Do you want to go for a brief minute?"

Go where? My silent question was answered with her hands. She pointed up, wanting me to look to my left at a point at ten o'clock on a clock face. There a doorway cut through the dark, and bright white light beamed down. Beyond the door an unseen choir sang and sweet fragrances wafted down, a subtle cross between the scent of a magnolia blossom and a gardenia.

The angel then pointed downward. My eyes followed her fingers and the line of a spotlight shone down into the Mississippi night. At the end of the light was my mangled body lying in a pool of blood. Below my shorts, my right leg was unnaturally twisted. My sandals were knocked off my feet.

I turned back to the angel and saw an overwhelming sorrow in her face. I felt the urge to reach up and wipe a tear from her cheek. When she saw my compassion, she said, "It's not your time, but do you want to come with me?"

I knew the choice was mine to make. "No," I quickly answered. "I want to stay with my husband and children."

"That's okay. It's not your time," she repeated. "You still have work to do."

With that, from the far end of a cave, I heard another familiar voice calling my name, louder and louder. "Linda. Linda. It's me, Herbie." I was back inside my body, sprawled face-down in the roadside gravel. My arms were spread out. My butt was sticking up in the air. My right leg was turned all the way around. And I felt the pain of external wounds: first, second, and third degree road burns from my waist down to the bottoms of my feet, from my body sliding on the road and in the rocks.

Though pained by a broken rib and compressed vertebrae, Herbie walked away from the accident. I didn't. Over the next few days in the critical care unit I heard details of my internal injuries: a crushed hip; my pelvis shattered like eggshells; multiple leg breaks—seven breaks above my right knee—and compressed vertebrae. And then Herbie stood over my bed, relaying a grim prognosis. "Babe," he said, "you need a lot of surgeries. A lot of repair. But…the doctors don't think you'll ever walk again."

I stared at him. Every broken and unbroken bone in my body revolted. I gritted my teeth and went to war. "No way," I said. "I'm going to lick this."

A sad smile fell across his face. He knew I was a fighter. But was my goal too ambitious?

Later Marla and Sandra tiptoed in, weepy and uncharacteristically quiet. "Mama?"

I had chosen life on this earth to complete my mission: to raise my daughters and make a home for my family. And I desperately wanted to assure my girls that we *were* a family. "Mom's here," I said. "I'm awake and I'm here for you. You'll have to help me out now—for a while—but I'll be back for you. Nothing is going to stop me from being there for you and your dad."

With my good arm I pulled Marla close, down onto the bed that was laced with tubes tied to machines. I ignored the nurse on the other side of the glass wall, eyeing us with disapproval. I held on to my dear one for dear life, and we cried together.

In those first days I didn't fully understand that my life still teetered on the brink of death. On Thursday evening I lay alone, half asleep, lulled by the morphine and the rhythmic bleep of the heart monitor rigged to my chest. But suddenly the rhythm stopped. I closed my eyes and drifted off. From afar I heard one extended *beeeeep* of the machine, and at that instant I saw my beautiful angel—she was smaller now, the size of a tall man— standing at the foot of my bed.

She wore the same white robes, still blown by an internal wind, still illuminated by an internal light. As she walked closer to me, she displaced the end of the bed; I could no longer see the traction pulley that supported my right leg, and yet the tension stayed taut.

Again her dainty hands spoke as clearly as her voice: "Linda, I'm here. You have a long way to go but I am with you. Things will be all right. There will be much to endure, but I will be with you."

I smiled at her and blinked my eyes in gratitude. I reached out my right hand to touch her, but with a smile on her face she faded like mist.

She was gone, and two wide-eyed nurses towered over my chest. One frantically checked the monitors. The other wielded electronic paddles that jolt a heart back to beating.

"Oh, Linda….We thought…the monitor…your heart flat-lined…cardiac arrest."

I heard what the nurses said, but I didn't reply with medical talk. "I saw her again," I said.

"Who, honey?"

"The angel."

"Where?"

"In here with me. She told me not to worry, that things would be all right."

That second angelic message has given me the strength to fight a battle that has raged longer and more fiercely than I ever imagined: fifty-eight days in the hospital; five months bedridden at home; six months in a wheelchair. I gained ground inch by inch—learning to sit, to stand, to take baby steps while clinging to a walker, to steady my gait with two canes, now with just one cane. I can't trudge through the woods or hike a hillside trail, but I can walk!

Every victory came with pain, which continues to taunt me. It hides deep in a bunker that I cannot dig out.

In the moment of the accident, my life changed forever. I will never again romp from one high-action activity to the next—playing ball with my children, running in the sand at the beach, trudging through thick woods.

And yet every morning I wake, thankful that my deepest prayers have been answered: In the face of death—at the time of the accident impact—I felt no pain. And with the gift of extended life on earth, I am able to guide and be a cheerleader for my family. This year Marla graduated from high school, and I was at the graduation. Sandra is in the band. And Herb—he's out back cleaning his gun, getting ready for opening day of deer season.

That guardian angel print still hangs over my bed, and remains my inspiration. It's a reminder of my own angel, and it inspires a new style in my painting. I no longer sketch unpeopled nature scenes. My paintings now tell stories—most often my story, which isn't complete without my guardian angel.

I portray my angel as I saw her, very different from the broad-winged angel of the traditional painting on my wall. My bright angel hovers in the dark. I struggle to capture the luminescence of her robe, the slight curve of her wrist, the silkiness of her skin. I can't get it quite right, but I keep going back to the sketch pad and easel, eager to try again to capture her essence—the love that overshadows any sorrow.

Since seeing my angel face to face, I've taken on another venture: For the first time in my life, I'm reading the Bible through, beginning to end. I want to know what it says about life and death, about humans and angels, about the Lord of the universe.

I shouldn't be surprised at what I read, but I am. From those ancient writers I find confirmation for my experience. Some of it is subtle, but it is there—in Psalm 55:6 (KJV): "Oh that I had wings like a dove! for then would I fly away, and be at rest." And in Psalm 36:9: "For with thee is the fountain of life: in thy light shall we see light."

And I was reminded that some women, men, and children have always been blessed to hear some nonhuman voice speak their names. "Hagar." "Samuel." "Zacharias." "Mary."

A few months ago, nearly two years after the accident, I was working on an angel painting. It was about time for me to go pick up my children from school, so I set my paints aside and soaked my brushes. I walked to the kitchen to wash my hands. Just as I had lathered them up, scrubbing at the paint, I heard my name called. "Linda, I am here!" The voice came from one of the bedrooms, down the hall.

Knowing it's hard for me to get in and out of a vehicle, the girls sometimes catch a ride home. *They must have come in,* I thought, eager to greet them. "I'll be right there, girls," I quickly answered. "I'm just cleaning up."

I rinsed and dried my hands and walked the length of the house, looking in each bedroom. No one was there. No TV. No radio. *But I heard a voice. A female voice. If not my kids, then who?*

Oh my! Yes, it was the same familiar voice. "I am here," she assured me. "I am here." *The God of Love will not leave me comfortless. His messenger is with me.*

I left to pick up the kids from school. We got back home before I told them I had heard my angel—right in our house, in one of the bedrooms, maybe theirs.

Neither Sandra nor Marla looked at me with disbelief. They smiled, reached arms around my shoulders, and whispered the words I'd lived to hear: "We love you, Mom. We're so glad you're here."

Marion S. Hodgson

"JUST A STAY-AT-HOME MAMA," is one way Marion Hodgson has described herself in the past. She and her husband Ned have lived in the same house in Fort Worth, Texas, since 1949, and they have reared their three children there, but "stay-at-home-mama" doesn't give a clue to this plucky woman's spirit of adventure. She has always looked at life as a dare.

Marion's father was the director of athletics at the University of Georgia in her hometown of Athens. He died at an early age during the Great Depression and after that there was precious little money for his widow, son and two daughters. Marion grabbed at every chance to get ahead. She graduated from high school at fifteen, worked for a degree in journalism at the university, did things like teaching herself shorthand and renting a typewriter for two dollars a month so she could learn to type on her own.

One unexpectedly significant thing she did was to enroll in a civilian pilot's training course. It was free to women and she got college credit for it. Since she was a minor, she needed her mother's permission to sign up, but her mother refused to give it. Only after Marion had enlisted the persuasive powers of an airline pilot, whose family were her family's friends, did her mother relent. In 1941, only months before the U.S. entered World War II, Marion received her pilot's license and her diploma the same month. She was nineteen.

Later, living in Chicago, using her secretarial skills at the War Department, she had one pleasant kind of hometown date with Ned Hodgson, the persuasive family friend, who had left the airlines and was then a Navy pilot. Shortly after that he crashed and was horribly burned in a Marine Corps plane. And soon after that Marion was recruited for Jacqueline Cochran's WASPs (Women Airforce Service Pilots). After six months of training in Sweetwater, Texas, she was flying open cockpit Fairchilds and Stearmans, ferrying AT-6s, C-45s and other Corps trainers from factories to air bases, releasing men for combat duty. At first she wrote Ned every day during his long stay in the hospital "just to cheer him up." The cheer turned into love, and, in 1944, marriage.

Recovered, but restricted to limited flight status, Ned was assigned to the Marine Corps Air Station in Fort Worth. Both Hodgsons liked the city, and after Ned left the service and went into the insurance business, that's where they stayed.

When it comes to spiritual matters, Marion has shown her mettle there, too. She admits that she was once an agnostic, partly because of resentment she felt when her beloved young father died; yet at a later time she took a bold step toward finding faith in Jesus. Even as a strong Christian believer, however, she was unaware of the reality of angels.

A friend, Edith Deen, author of *All the Women of the Bible*, casually included angels in her conversation with Marion one morning, just as though they were real. "I was shocked," Marion says. "I didn't believe they were. I didn't know what the Bible said about them."

That shock set her thinking, and before long, after recalling a series of events that were not to be explained in human terms, she had to admit that angels must be what Edith Deen said they were—present today. Marion had never forgotten the close call when she and another WASP and nineteen servicemen were passengers sitting in a DC-3 at LaGuardia Airport in New York. No sooner had the plane taken off and climbed to three hundred feet, when first one, then the other engine, went dead (it's a ten million to one chance that two engines should die simultaneously). With a number of quick, desperate maneuvers, the pilot got the plane turned around, the wheels down, high tension wires missed, and all lives saved.

"But he did all the wrong things," Marion recalls. "He broke all the rules he'd been taught. Why? Because a 'voice' had directed him to do them? I believe now that angels *were* with us."

The stay-at-home mama is still there in the house where a family of armadillos often wanders by the front yard and a raccoon insists upon eating his lunch on their roof. Ned is retired. He likes to read and garden; Marion likes to write (she's had four cookbooks published as well as short stories in *McCall's* and *Good Housekeeping*, and most recently the Naval Institute has accepted *WASP: A Woman Airforce Service Pilot in World War II*, Marion and Ned's wartime correspondence). They both like to travel abroad, but wherever they are, every morning they hold hands when they pray. "And we always ask God to keep His angels watching over our family," Marion says.

The End of the Line

by Marion S. Hodgson

Give to the winds thy fears,
Hope, and be undismayed;
God hears thy sighs, and counts thy tears,
God shall lift up thy head.
Through waves and clouds and storms
he gently clears the way;
Wait thou his time, so shall the night
Soon end in joyous day.

Far, far above thy thought
His counsel shall appear,
When fully he the work hath wrought
That caused thy needless fear.
Leave to his sovereign will
To choose and to command:
With wonder filled, thou then shalt own
How wise, how strong his hand.

—Paul Gerhardt, *translated by John Wesley*

Y FRIENDS USED TO TELL ME I was an overly protective mother. I always bristled at the phrase. Hadn't I been temporarily entrusted with something unutterably precious—children? How could a mother be too careful?

To me, motherhood was the most delightful, if sometimes exhausting and frustrating, career I could imagine. Actually, I was an agnostic until the moment a nurse placed my first child in my arms. The gift of life suddenly proved the existence of a heavenly Giver of Life.

And fifteen years later, a motherly concern that my family of five worship together drove me to confirmation classes. Although I believed in God, there was so much else in the ancient Christian creed: the Trinity, a virgin birth, a resurrection, and my own redemption. I went through the course twice, unconvinced. Finally I talked to the minister. "How can I say I believe in the deity of Jesus—when I don't?"

His answer? Relax and take the next step.

He scheduled a private baptism service, and I arrived at the church in an agonized state. During the service I stood next to my husband Ned and begged God's forgiveness: "Forgive me for what I'm about to say: that I believe, when I don't."

As my pain consumed me, something unexplainable happened. I can only say that I was zapped by God, by Jesus. It was as if an electrical current flashed through my blood. I knew Jesus was with me and *in* me. I knew the Bible, which I'd laughed at all my life, was true.

From that day on, I couldn't get enough of God's Word. I devoured it, claiming one particular verse as my own: "He who is in you is greater than he who is in the world" (1 John 4:4, NKJV).

Our twelve-year-old daughter Marjorie sensed a change in me: I was more patient with the children and with my mother who was virtually deaf. Marjorie's own interest in the Bible intensified, and soon we prayed together regularly; to this day we're prayer partners.

In time, Marjorie left home for Texas Tech, where she fell in love her senior year with the rancher of her dreams, Joe Parker. And over her Christmas break, the winter of 1972-73, she begged to borrow my '65 Mustang and drive nearly three hours north from Fort Worth to Joe's ranch for a weekend with him and his parents.

The request wasn't unreasonable, except that North Texas was locked in ice. And my trusty Mustang had an inadequate heater. I thought my lovesick daughter had lost her mind. "Marjorie," I said, "it's well below freezing. The roads will be treacherous. You'd freeze to death. You'll have to call Joe and tell him you can't come."

"But Joe says that the highway patrol says that the roads are okay between here and Jacksboro. That's halfway. I could leave your car there; Joe will meet me at the Green Frog Cafe, and we'll go the rest of the way in his four-wheel-drive truck. Trust me, Mom. Everything will be okay."

"Honey, Jacksboro is nearly an hour and a half away," I reminded her. "The heater in the Mustang doesn't work worth a toot in this kind of weather. I tell you, you'd freeze."

I was tempted to call Ned at his office, for moral support. But I knew how pressured he was, and I hated to bother him. Surely I could talk some sense into Marjorie.

Her mind was set. "I can wear my ski clothes," she said. "And I can put cardboard in front of Musty's radiator. Remember how we did that last winter when we went skiing?" Her blue eyes were pleading.

"Yes, but then we hadn't just had an ice storm."

"The traffic between here and Jacksboro has worn all the ice off the highway. They say you just have to be careful on overpasses and bridges. And they *always* say that."

"And with good reason. Marge, you just can't go. You'll be back at Texas Tech with Joe in two weeks. Surely you can stand being separated that long."

The blue eyes turned black with emotion, pupils dilated. "Mom, I haven't seen him for two weeks. I'll die if I have to wait two more." She burst into tears.

I agonized, remembering what it was like to be young and wildly in love, when a month of separation seemed like a lifetime. Was I being rational or unreasonable? So, okay, I took my responsibilities as a mother seriously. Was that being overprotective? On the one hand, Marjorie *was* twenty-one years old. On the other hand, wasn't she still my responsibility as long as she was in school? And whose car was she asking to borrow?

But those big black eyes. I did hate to break her heart. Joe would be disappointed too, and I was crazy about my future son-in-law. "Tell you what," I said. "I'll take you as far as Jacksboro and then turn around and bring Musty back home. I've had more experience driving on ice, in case we hit some."

"Oh, Mom, thank you! Thank you!" She threw her arms around my neck. I hugged her waist; she felt so slim and fragile that I felt, well, overprotective.

I left a note for Ned, telling him I'd be back in plenty of time for the dinner party we were going to.

As I donned ski clothes and warm boots, I wondered if I had lost my mind, too. Marjorie and I wedged cardboard in front of the Mustang's radiator to block off some of the cold air and keep us a little warmer. I turned the ignition key and headed north.

The roads were clear enough at first, the traffic having dissipated the sheet of ice. But once on the Jacksboro highway, the traffic thinned out. Even so, we didn't encounter any ice on the road, and soon we were jabbering like schoolgirls on a picnic. Not that the frozen landscape invited such warm thoughts: Texas mesquite and scrub oaks dotted the fields split and gullied by washes. Occasional clusters of cattle huddled miserably, waiting for a ranch hand to come throw them some hay from a truck. A horsehead oil drill stood silent, as if frozen immobile.

After we'd been on the road for an hour, I knew my toes were turning blue, in spite of the fur-lined boots. And we were virtually alone on the road. It was dry and clear—but where was everybody? Had this trip been a mistake? While I ruminated, I let Marjorie do more of the talking. About ten miles from Jacksboro, I heaved a sigh of relief at the sight of a Lone Star Gas compressor station. Four parked trucks and a billowing smokestack assured me we weren't the only humans in the desolate countryside.

But a mile later, as the cold was biting my bones, I said, "Marjo, we were foolish to take a chance on a day like this."

But lovesick Marjorie didn't seem to mind the chill or the isolated winter road. "We're nearly there, Mom. And look! There are two cars ahead."

So there were, climbing a long hill—and sliding crazily back and forth across the two northbound lanes.

"Look at those idiot drivers," I exclaimed. "They don't know how to drive on ice." But the words were hardly out of my mouth, when my wheels hit the invisible ice.

None of the standard tricks for driving on ice worked. I lost control instantly and couldn't get it back: I didn't steer against the skid or apply my brakes. I even accelerated slightly, since we were going uphill.

The Mustang side-slipped over both northbound lanes, then spun across the solid line, in front of a car heading toward us over the crest of the hill. By the grace of God, we didn't collide. We did a 180-degree turn, slid off the west shoulder of the road, and stopped in a deep rut in a frozen field.

We'd slid so fast I hadn't had time to pray. But now that we were stopped, I let out a big sigh: "TYG and TYJ"—our family contraction for "Thank you, God, and thank you, Jesus."

"Amen!" answered Marjorie. Then, "Mom, you okay?"

"Whew. Yes. You?"

She nodded and we sat for a brief moment to get our bearings and breath. I proposed a revised plan. "We'll just drive back to that Lone Star Gas place. We'll call Joe at the Green Frog and ask him to come pick you up at Lone Star. I'm not tackling that hill again."

But when I tried to drive out of the field, the back wheels spun...and spun. "Let's see if we can make some traction," I suggested, remembering that sticks and straw placed under back wheels sometimes helped. But the icy spikes we broke off didn't look too promising. Still, we tried. Climbing back in the car, we held hands and offered a quick prayer of thanks that we hadn't been injured. "And Lord," I continued, "we pray that You will help us get the car back on the road—and to safety."

With new confidence, I tried to pull out. Nothing doing. We spun. We rocked. We sat. Shivering, we stopped and prayed again, more fervently. But we just sank deeper into the icy rut.

Marjorie and I looked at each other. With a twinkle in her eyes, she asked me if I might be harboring some unconfessed sin that would be blocking my prayer. My conscience clean, I jokingly asked the same question of her. We again grasped each other's gloved hands. "Dear Lord," I spoke very loudly, "here we are again, two of us in agreement. You promised You would be with us and give us whatever we asked for, in faith, in Jesus' name, in accordance with Your will. Can it be Your will that we freeze out here in this field? We're confused that You haven't answered, but we ask again in faith. We need Your help. We're cold. We're stuck. Help us! You promised!"

Before I'd said amen, a battered old car appeared from nowhere. Heading south, it pulled off the road and slid to a stop behind us in the frozen field.

Expecting supernatural intervention, not earthly help, I frantically waved for it to drive on. "Don't stop," I futilely shouted out the window. "You'll never get out of here."

But two fortyish men were already stopped and walking toward us. They looked like typical Texas ranchers, dressed for the cold: ruddy faces framed by fleece-lined caps; bodies encased in quilted, down-filled jackets; Levis pulled down over the tops of their boots.

"Oh, you shouldn't have stopped. But thank you, I'm sure glad you did." I didn't for a second think of being afraid of them. We had prayed so diligently; the road was too treacherous for anyone to harm us and make a quick getaway.

"Don't worry about us, ma'am," said the taller of the two Good Samaritans. "We'll be okay. Let me get behind the wheel and see if I can get you out of this fix."

I slid over and nearly squeezed Marjorie off her bucket seat.

The second man pushed down on the trunk, while the driver slowly accelerated. The wheels whirred and spun, stopped, then whirred again. We hadn't budged.

The driver opened his door. "We'll both put our weight over the back wheels and push," he explained. Nodding at me, he continued, "You take the wheel. Just drive straight ahead and don't cut your wheels. Don't even try to angle toward the highway until you are really moving. Aim straight ahead. Don't try to look back and wave or thank us. When you have everything under control, just ease back onto the highway—when nobody's coming."

He nodded toward Marjorie. "You, Miss. You watch for cars. She needs to keep her eyes on where she's going. Then when the car is moving straight ahead under control, you tell her if it's okay to ease toward the road."

"But what about you?" I asked. "How will you get out of here?"

"Don't worry about us, Ma'am. This is the end of the line for us."

At the time I didn't think about what he might have meant. I just sputtered, "I don't know how to thank you." I didn't feel right about reaching for my purse; they didn't seem like the kind of men who would accept money.

He touched his hand to his cap, smiled, and walked around to the Mustang's rear, where his partner waited. Each put his weight over one of the back wheels and pushed mightily while I gingerly accelerated.

It worked! The wheels caught, the car inched forward, then kept moving—straight ahead. I let out a war whoop. "Wave to them, Marge. Wave! Blow kisses! We're home free!" I edged toward the highway, which she assured me was empty.

Marjorie turned around to wave. Her hand stopped in midair.

"Wave, honey, wave!" I shouted. "Thank them! Hallelujah! Oh, TYG and TYJ."

"Mother." She was strangely subdued and quiet.

"What?"

"Mother, you're not going to believe this." She was whispering.

"What is it?" I tried to see in the rear view mirror what was going on.

"No one is there. They've disappeared."

I kept the car straight, even as I searched for the car in the mirror. They were gone. No car. No men. The field and the highway were deserted.

Marge searched the road for logical explanations. "They couldn't have turned around, because there's no one on the hill. And they didn't pass us. There's a little road behind us on the right leading into that pasture. But it has a gate and it's shut. They didn't have time to get as far as that gate, anyway, much less open and close it. Besides, I can see the road beyond the gate, and there's no car on it. What's going on, Mother?"

Goose bumps ran down my arms as the words came to my lips. "They were angels, Marge, angels."

"Oh, Mother, there's got to be some other explanation."

"Well?"

She couldn't come up with a better explanation. Neither could I.

We got back to the Lone Star Gas compressor station with no problem, on a dry road, and within the hour Marjorie was jumping in the front seat of Joe's truck, waving good-bye as she rode toasty-warm, north into the frozen Texas countryside.

After warming up inside the station, I headed back south toward Fort Worth. I tried to make sense of the cryptic phrase, "This is the end of the line for us." What did it mean? Again I could see only one explanation: They'd accomplished the mission they'd been sent to perform.

That may have been true, and yet I drove home with the full assurance that unseen angelic beings were still present with me and with Marjorie. More important, their Commander was still present in me and in Marjorie. With such a team at hand, could I trust our future—my daughter's future—to our heavenly Father's good care? Yes, a load of worry lifted. TYG and TYJ!

Marjorie and Joe's wedding date was set for June, as soon as the wheat would be harvested. It was a bright clear Saturday, and in the church brides' room, minutes before I was to walk that aisle and take my front-row seat, Marjorie and I held hands for one last prayer together as mother and unmarried daughter. Things would never be exactly the same. She was an adult now, cleaving to a husband whose home and life would be hers. We would still be close—always mother and daughter—but you might say I'd accomplished the mission I'd been sent to perform. In a sense this was the end of the line for us.

Marjorie also sensed that her joyous new beginning was linked to a nostalgic ending. Both teary-eyed, we bowed our heads and in a strangled voice I whispered, "O God, help us, help us get through this ceremony without breaking down and making fools of ourselves. Thank You for our wonderful years together and may You bless Marjorie's new life with Joe. May You be glorified in this ceremony."

Marjorie and I opened our eyes and both of us broke into big smiles. In that prayer, God had eased our tension and filled us with his peace and calm. I didn't actually say the words, but we both knew our journey together wasn't over. *My mission may be accomplished, Marge. It's time for me to step out of the picture, but I'm still here. I'm still your mom.*

I kissed her cheek and we headed for the door to the church sanctuary. Still smiling, I walked down the aisle on a groomsman's arm. Out of the corner of my eye, on the groom's side, I noticed row after row of cowboy boots sticking out beneath Sunday suits.

I wouldn't have been surprised to recognize two ruddy-faced, fortyish ranchers seated in a pew. Though I didn't see them, I knew God's messengers were present, encouraging me to release my daughter into God's—and Joe's—loving care.

Years later, when Marjorie asked if I could stay with my two preschool grandchildren while she and Joe attended a three-day cattlemen's convention, I gave a quick, "Yes, I can come up." Yes, I still had a role to play in my daughter's life.

The next week I drove my trusty little Musty north on the Jacksboro highway. And just beyond that Lone Star Gas compressor station, I thought about those two ranchers who pulled up in that jalopy just to push us out of a ditch. As I started up the slight incline I said, *This is it. This is where I skidded into the field.*

I spontaneously broke out in praise, quoting my favorite verse: "He who is in you is greater than he who is in the world" (1 John 4:4).

As soon as I finished the sentence, the Mustang shuddered violently. It felt as if the car were a rag doll being shaken in a dog's jowls. *Oh dear, I've blown a tire.* No. The steering wasn't out of control. *It's something under the hood.* As I looked for a safe place to pull off the road, I passed beyond the "miracle spot"—and the quaking stopped, never to return, though I still drive my vintage Mustang around Fort Worth.

I say the quaking stopped—in the car. But in my heart? I still shiver and get goose bumps down my arms when I talk about that winter day, when two ranchers pushed us out of an icy rut and disappeared. It may have been the end of the line for them, but for me as a mother it was the beginning of a peaceful ride.

"TYG and TYJ."

Dennis Tyrone Jodouin

THE PHOTOGRAPH OF DENNIS TYRONE JODOUIN was taken at the time of this story in 1984. It shows him dressed in his uniform as a lieutenant in Toledo, Ohio's Fire Department, standing in front of Engine House No. 19's fire truck. He retired recently at the age of fifty-five after twenty-seven years and seven months of service. These were years in which, not unlike firemen everywhere, his life was often in jeopardy. Only once does he feel that he was in a hopeless situation. "That was because of my mistake," he has said, "a mistake I never made again." You'll read about it here in "Two Minutes to Live."

Ty Jodouin (his friends call him "Ty"—his mother was a fan of the movie star Tyrone Power) was born in Timmins, a small town far up in Ontario, Canada. He's lived in the United States since he was six, was educated in Toledo schools (Waite High), spent two years on active naval duty mostly aboard USS *Des Moines*, flagship of the Sixth Fleet, then eight years in the Naval Reserve. Back in civilian clothes, he apprenticed himself to a printer for a while, worked up to journeyman, then the fire department called. During all those years, however, Ty had another career in mind.

Ty wanted to be a writer. It wasn't just a pipe dream. He worked at it, taking workshop courses at the University of Toledo, spending long, off-duty hours at his computer. He wrote a book—it took him four years—and now that book has been published by Northwest Publishing, Inc., Salt Lake City. The title? *Rogue Planet*.

Ty's mother used to tell him often that he had been assigned a guardian angel at birth. It took him a long time to believe her. Even an unnerving experience he'd had back in the days when he was an impulsive, carefree bachelor didn't make him think that his angel might be involved. Ty had a habit then of sleeping until the last minute on a working day, then hurrying out of the house, jumping in his car and barreling down to his favorite coffee shop. One morning he was racing down the street at fifty miles an hour when—

"Slow down." He had no idea where the words came from, but there was no doubt that they were there, and not just stray, unimportant words either; they had the force of a command that made him take his foot off the accelerator just as two little boys dashed out into the street chasing a ball. Ty stopped his car and broke out into a cold sweat.

Years later, when his own life was spared in his one "hopeless situation," Ty was ready to think seriously about the angel his mother had told him about so often. "Too many of us don't take much stock in angels until something actually happens to us personally," Ty says today. "But when it happens, you become a believer. You can't think about it logically, you just have to believe."

Ty and his wife Helen are members of Reformation Lutheran Church in Toledo where they have attended numerous Bible study classes in an effort to

148

learn still more about their religion and their Creator. Now, for the years ahead, he will go on writing, and he's determined to do some traveling. He'd like especially to show Helen the Mediterranean, which he first saw as a yeoman in the Sixth Fleet.

Two Minutes to Live

by Ty Jodouin

Whether you turn to the right
or to the left, your ears will
hear a voice behind you, saying,
"This is the way; walk in it."

—Isaiah 30:21 (NIV)

USED TO THINK I WAS LUCKY. As a lieutenant in the Toledo, Ohio, fire department I've had water-laden ceilings fall on my head, I've been blown down by explosions, I've fallen through floors eaten by fire. But after December 5, 1984, I've had to question how much was really luck. Maybe my mother was right when she told us children that each of us had his own guardian angel.

At Engine House No. 19 on that particular December morning, we checked our equipment as usual, paying special attention to our face masks. Smoke is the fire fighter's principal enemy, and we always make sure every valve is working, every air tank full. Then, at 10:43, the alarm sounded. As our pumper raced to the call at Chestnut and Noble, I wondered if everyone had got out safely. If they had, our job was to try to save the building.

Our truck approached the corner. Other pumpers were laying in hoses from a hydrant, their crews stretching the lines to the front and rear of the frame

151

duplex. Just as we pulled up, a violent back-draft explosion blew out the building's storefront window. Glass flew onto the crumbling concrete stoop. Black, rolling smoke vented from the hole. I ordered my crew to mask up.

We were beginning to pull hose off the pumper when the chief ran over to me. "Get upstairs quick, Lieutenant!" he said. "Use the back way. There's been screaming reported coming from up there."

Now it was a different ball game: We were no longer just fighting a fire, we were looking for a person trapped inside. I looked around at our new man, Bill.

"Let's go," I said. On the way, because he was a rookie, I briefed him. We'd climb the outside stairs, gain entrance to the second floor and feel our way through the smoke in the upstairs apartment, looking for a survivor. "Remember your training now," I said, little thinking that within moments I'd forget my own seventeen years of experience.

We raced up the outside stairs to the landing, paused, slipped on the face-pieces of our masks and turned on the valves. There was a hiss as compressed air flowed from the tank on my back through the tube into my mask. We'd have about twenty minutes before the air gave out.

"Okay, stay close to me," I said to Bill, my voice sounding muffled as it came through the mask's speaking diaphragm. We headed inside.

The first room we came to was filled with black, black smoke. I switched on my hand light. It didn't begin to penetrate the darkness. Following procedure, I started moving to my right, feeling my way around the wall. A stove, a refrigerator, and then an empty space. A doorway!

"Wait," I said, talking into the smoke. I could hardly see Bill. We stopped and listened, but the only sound was the muffled noise of fire fighters from the street below.

Our proper procedure was clear. Crouching into a semicrawl, we went through the doorway into the room off the kitchen, keeping contact with the wall on our right. I kept locating the wall with my foot, then I stretched into the middle of the room feeling for a human form. I touched pieces of furniture: a sofa, a chair, a cabinet. Then, on the floor, a heap of clothes. Was that a body? No, just clothes.

A bright blur ahead. A window. With the butt of my hand light I burst the glass; a surge of black smoke rushed past me into the open. I kept on. *Wheeze. Wheeze.* I could hear Bill behind me, drawing air into his mask.

Perspiration was running in a steady stream down my face and neck, stinging my eyes. The intense heat on my neck was a constant reminder that the fire was getting closer, racing up inside the walls. I skirted a bookcase, came to a corner, turned left, following the wall. Inch by inch I groped in the darkness, searching for what, I didn't know. Except for our own wheezing breath I hadn't heard a sound in the apartment since we began the search. Now little orange fragments started falling from the ceiling. Bad news: The fire was so hot it had ignited the plaster. Bits and pieces of it were floating down from the ceiling like deadly fireflies. I touched the wall again. Even through my gloves it was hot. We had to hurry!

Suddenly, I wasn't getting enough air. I inhaled more deeply. My tank couldn't be empty—we hadn't been in the building ten minutes. The warning bell in my equipment hadn't rung. I remembered procedure, reached for the emergency bypass valve and cranked it two turns. Nothing.

"Bill," I yelled into the blackness, "I've got trouble with my air." I tried to keep my muffled voice calm, but I heard a trace of panic in it. Without air, I had one, at the most two, minutes to live.

And then I made my first mistake. I did something totally *against* procedure and I ignored the first rule of safety of the fire fighter: Use the buddy system. In an emergency, you can share your partner's supply of air until you are out of danger. But instead I ordered the rookie fireman away. "Go back the way we came and get me another tank," I shouted. "I'll meet you at the landing."

Bill had scarcely left when I began to choke. Now panic took an iron hold and I made my second mistake. My only thought was to get air. The quickest way was to go straight to the door without circling the wall as I should have done. I stood up and ran.

I bumped into a table. A sofa. Another table. I ran forward, hit a chair, turned back, grasped my valve and turned it again. Nothing. My lungs burned. I sucked harder but there was just no air. Where was that door! Words came from training: "Don't forget," the drill instructors had preached, "you always have air trapped inside your clothing."

Gasping, I fell to the floor, disconnected my inhalation tube from the oxygen tank and stuck it inside my coat. Praying. A few more moments of life. Let there be air inside my fire coat!

I sucked hard. A precious bit of air came through! The smoke tasted hot, acrid, but the air was still breathable. I had bought another minute. I forced myself back up onto my hands and knees and started crawling through the obstacle course, under a table, over a stuffed chair. There was no way out now and I knew it. I started crying. With the same strange logic I had used in sending Bill away, I blamed God for my mistakes. Over and over the thought repeated itself, irrationally, insistently: *Dear God, why are You doing this to me? You know I'm getting married soon. I have so much to live for!*

Then I heard the voice, a whisper: "Look up! Look up!"

I barely moved my head, turning to the right. The voice came again, more insistently, "Not to your right, look to your left!"

The voice came more clearly now, as if through a megaphone in my ear, pressuring me as I felt my reactions slowing down. "To you left. Look up to your left! Don't you see it?"

Yes, I saw it! Through the blackness I barely made out a small fuzzy zone of light.

In slow motion I got up and started toward it, stumbling, falling. The light became a faint outline, then a distinct form. It was a window. The same window I had burst earlier.

I ripped off my mask and forced my body halfway through the frame into the fresh air outside. Again and again I drew clean air into my lungs, relishing the sounds of men below.

Then Bill was at my side. He helped me down the stairs to the street, where I learned that trouble with my equipment was a faulty valve. The cry from inside the building had been a cat, which unfortunately had not escaped. But not one person's life was lost—including my own!

When my mother used to tell me about my guardian angel, she had good scriptural backing. Jesus says about children, "I tell you that their angels in heaven always see the face of My Father in heaven" (Matthew 18:10, NIV).

Does a child's angel stay with him always, constantly regarding the face of the Father...even when, as an adult, he may forget to look up to God?

Today that is a question I no longer ask. I am satisfied it was my own angel who whispered to me, "Look up!"

Wally Metts

EARLY ON WALLY METTS SET HIS SIGHTS on being a doctor. At the age of sixteen he entered Tennessee Temple University; he later transferred to the University of Tennessee at Chattanooga where he majored in chemistry and biology. For years he did everything he could to qualify himself for admission to medical school, including a career in a hospital as a respiratory therapist. Wally never got to be a physician, but he did get to be a doctor. In 1995 he received his Ph.D. degree from Michigan State University. It seems that all the while what he really wanted to do with his life was to be a teacher.

Dr. Metts is now Professor of Communications at Spring Arbor College in Spring Arbor, Michigan. He found his way there after a stint at teaching fifth and sixth grades in a Christian academy—that's when he discovered that he really loved academia—and five years more of teaching at Tennessee Temple.

Then came his master's degree in English education from the University of Knoxville. He met his wife Katie way back in his sixteen-year-old freshman days at Tennessee Temple; they were married in 1974. She was a Yankee from Michigan, a fact that had something to do with his heading north for a position at Spring Arbor.

While Katie is a Yankee from Michigan, Wally is a bonafide Cracker from Florida. His family has been in the Sunshine State for five generations. Wally's father, Wally Metts, Senior, was pastor of Russell Park Baptist Church in Fort Myers, where Wally grew up as a preacher's kid who helped out in church by playing the piano and organ.

"We were pretty conservative," Wally says about his family and his upbringing. "No dancing, and I didn't see a movie in a theater until I was thirty."

Back in those days his family and friends called him "Sailor," a nickname derived somehow from his mother's love for fishing in the waters of the Gulf.

Wally and Katie have four children, Margaret, Christian, Michael, and Pilgrim. The family lives in the country with a garden plot and chickens, two cats, and a German shepherd called Mariel. All four of the Metts children attend school right there at home, with Katie shouldering most of the teaching load. This was something that the Mettses decided to do long before home schooling became a movement.

Wally has been a newspaper correspondent and columnist for the *Jackson Citizen Patriot*, where he still does an occasional feature, and he's an associate editor on the staff of *Guideposts for Kids*. What name does he use for his articles in that publication? Answer: Sailor Metts.

The Vigil

by Sailor Metts

Let us help each other
by our prayers,
so that God and Christ
and the whole choir of angels,
may come to our aid
in our time of suffering,
when we shall need their
assistance the most.

—Nemesian of Numidia

HE CAT WOKE ME, nudging my face with her nose.
I sat up quickly, instantly alert. Something was wrong. I'm a sound sleeper, not easily roused. And Katie usually lets the cat out, not me.

I looked at the clock. It was 1:45 A.M., but Katie wasn't in bed beside me. The house was dark except for the blinking lights of the Christmas tree in the living room. It was a small house; I immediately knew she wasn't home yet. She had gone to town to study for a philosophy test with a friend. She should have been back long ago.

Through the wall I could hear the branch of a large elm tree scraping

against the vinyl siding. A harsh wind seeped in around the edges of our inex-
pensive—and ineffective—storm windows.

I looked at Christian, our five-year-old sleeping soundly at my side. He still
climbed in bed with us sometimes in the middle of the night; eventually Katie
would carry him back to his own room or nudge me awake and get me to do
it. I have to admit that I sometimes played possum.

I wasn't playing possum now.

Michael had climbed onto our bed about 9:30. I had lain down with him to
get him to go to sleep, and I had fallen asleep myself. As I looked down at
Michael, I petted the cat absently, ignoring her plea.

The room seemed strangely light, so I glanced out the window. I couldn't
see the moon or any stars. But down the hill in the backyard the ground was
covered with snow. It was still coming down, whipping past the window. At
the sight of the white film on the grass, I began to pray for Katie. It's something I don't do nearly enough.

And within seconds the cat jumped off the bed, trying to lead me to the
kitchen door. I picked Christian up and followed the cat down the hall, stopping to put him in his bed and pull the covers up around his shoulders. Margaret's room was at the end of the hall near the kitchen; I looked in on her,
too. She was seven, with a fair, pristine beauty. A princess, I thought. But of
course I'm her dad.

Then I opened the door and let the cat out into the garage where she'd find
her cat box, water, food, whatever it was she wanted.

What I myself wanted was for Katie to be home, now, before the snow
accumulated. We'd moved to Michigan from Tennessee two years before, and
Katie was still not very confident about driving in the snow. Even though she
grew up in Michigan, and I in south Florida, she let me drive at the threat of

bad weather. And now, in mid-December, I had not yet put the snow tires on our old Fairmont station wagon.

I walked down the hall to the living room and stood beside the Christmas tree. As usual, Katie had picked out a tree only a mother could love. Sometimes I think she has compassion even for plants. It was crooked and short, but we'd picked it out and cut it down ourselves at a nearby tree farm, and the kids had been tickled. That was over a week ago, the first Sunday of Advent. We had invited some college students over to string popcorn and cranberries, and then I had put on the lights. Before Meg and Christian hung the ornaments they had made or we had collected over the years, I placed a small, white plastic angel in a circle of flashing lights on the top of Katie's crooked tree.

It was no high-fashion angel. I had bought it at Walgreen's the year after we had married. But for precisely that reason it was worth a lot. And it reminded me, somehow, of a song at the center of my Southern childhood, an old spiritual: "All night, all day, angels watching over me, my Lord." My dad had sung it as a lullaby. My mom had assured me it was true. I had heard it in my home— and in my heart.

I stood beside the tree and looked out the double windows toward the road. The branches of the two large cedar pines in the front yard were not snowy white. It was too windy, the snow too fine. I convinced myself it didn't look bad.

I went back to the kitchen, out into the garage, and I opened the door to the driveway. I picked up the broom and brushed the wispy snow—to discover that it covered a sheet of ice. Apparently the drizzle, which had started shortly after Katie had left at 6:30, had turned to freezing rain and then snow. It was worse than it looked.

Katie's friend Kathy lived right on the Spring Arbor College campus. The commute to our rural home was six miles by the unpaved back roads, eight miles by "main" roads, which were still fairly isolated. I'd clocked this myself, because I teach at the college. I could imagine too many scenarios of what might have happened to Katie, driving on this ice over the rolling hills.

But then, I reasoned, maybe Katie and Kathy—such diligent, compulsive students—were still poring over their philosophy notes, preparing for that final exam. I went back inside to call Kathy, whose husband was also a faculty member.

"Hi, Kathy. This is Wally. Is Katie there?"

"She left ten or fifteen minutes ago," she said. "She isn't home yet?"

"No," I said. "I hope she didn't take the back roads." I was thinking of the corner of Bowerman and Matthews Roads. The turn, at the top of a hill, was always treacherous in bad weather.

I promised to call her back if there was a problem. I looked at the clock. I hung up the phone at 1:55. And I suddenly felt an urge to pray with great earnestness. As I prayed I did the things a man does when his wife may be stranded on a winter road: I mentally calculated time and distance, wondered if I should leave the kids and go look for her; wondered how soon I should call the police.

"Please, Lord. Please bring her home," I prayed. As I paced the living room floor, the lights strung around the window reflected an icy glaze framing a winter scene that seemed more ominous by the minute. The lights on the Christmas tree, all white, flashed off and on. I looked up at the white angel standing vigil at the top of the tree. The song was true: There were angels watching over me, and over Katie.

The minutes dragged by. At last Katie's car pulled in the drive, and Katie got out. There have been few times when I was more glad to see her. She was shivering. I pulled her small body to me and buried my head in her auburn hair.

I helped her get her coat off, and we walked into the living room where we sat down together and she began to tell me about her drive home. Katie had taken the back roads and had lost control of the car, skidding into a deep ditch—at Bowerman and Matthews.

"I was stuck," she told me. "I tried to push the car out. I tried to rock it out. The tires just kept spinning, digging in deeper and deeper. I was about to walk home," she continued, "but I was too scared." The intersection was three miles from the house, down a deserted gravel road.

At 1:55, just before she was going to get out and walk, she decided to try to rock the car out one more time, and again it was hopeless. The tires were spinning on a sheet of ice.

"But suddenly," she continued, "it felt like someone just picked up the back end of the car and set it down on the road. I drove the rest of the way carefully, and here I am."

I've thought about that night many times since then. I thought about it two years later when Katie turned that same car over on a busy freeway—and she and the kids walked away unscratched. And I've thought about it this year as our daughter, now sixteen, faces her first winter behind the wheel.

And, of course, I think about it every Christmas, when angels seem to be everywhere. And especially when we take out the little white plastic angel and put it in its accustomed place at the highest point of our tree.

❧

Everlasting God, you have ordained and constituted in a wonderful order the ministries of angels and mortals: Mercifully grant that, as your holy angels always serve and worship you in heaven, so by your appointment they may help and defend us here on earth; through Jesus Christ our Lord, who lives and reigns with you and the Holy Spirit, one God, for ever and ever. Amen.

—*The Book of Common Prayer,*
prayer for the feast of St. Michael and All Angels

⤜ Anna Loomis ⤛

ANNA LOOMIS HAS DONE A FAIR AMOUNT OF TRAVELING since she was born in the city of Tilburg, Netherlands, just before the beginning of World War II. As a young woman she toured Europe as a singer in a band. Her favorite uncle had an orchestra, and one night his vocalist came down with laryngitis; Anna stepped in as a substitute and never stepped out. She loved singing the American-type music that the orchestra played, the kind of music she was singing when she met and fell in love with an American serving overseas in the Air Force. They were married and lived in England where he was stationed. They had three children, two boys and a girl.

When her young husband was killed in a car crash, Anna brought her children to his parents' home in Wellsboro, Pennsylvania, for the funeral. That is where she and Tom Loomis met and how she happened to live first in Kentucky, and eventually on the five acres of land in upstate New York that the Loomis family calls home today.

The Netherlands, England, New York—a great deal of geography covered, but nothing to compare with the vast spiritual territory she has crossed in the journey she writes about here.

"I was not a Christian when Tom and I were married," Anna has said. "I knew nothing about religion or God or whatever. It wasn't a part of my upbringing, not at all. Back then Tom and I never even mentioned the subject. As a kid he had been dragged to church so often that I think he was numb by the time he became an adult. No, God simply wasn't there for either of us."

Hard to believe that those words could have come from a woman who has had so many spiritual adventures that when the extraordinary encounter with a giant being she describes here happened, she was afraid to tell even her trusting husband; she feared he would not believe her. Later, on a visit to Washington, D.C., quite by chance she read a book that Sophy Burnham had written about angels. Suddenly all kinds of bells went off in her head. She picked up a telephone, somehow got through immediately to the author, and blurted out the event that Mrs. Burnham would relate in her fascinating book, *Angel Letters*. Anna tells the rest of her adventure now. It ends with the appearance of an angel who comes for a purely spiritual purpose: to bring Anna into a new realm of worship and praise.

A Light, a Voice, and a Flight

by Anna Loomis

May none of God's wonderful works
keep silence, night or morning.
Bright stars, high mountains, the depths of the seas,
sources of rushing rivers:
may all these break into song as we sing
to Father, Son, and Holy Spirit.
May all the angels in the heavens reply:
Amen! Amen! Amen!
Power, praise, honour, eternal glory
to God, the only Giver of grace.
Amen! Amen! Amen!

—A Third-Century Egyptian Doxology

WHEN TOM LOOMIS AND I WERE MARRIED, he was a widower with three children and I a widow who had three children. We went to live in Harrodsburg, Kentucky, where he worked as an engineering representative for Corning, the glass-making company. After two years I came to the sad conclusion that our marriage simply wasn't right. Tom was always on the road and I was always at home, washing clothes, feeding hungry faces, chauffeuring children. Life was so different from what I was used to. I wanted to break away, take myself back to Holland where I came from, maybe go back to making my living as a singer.

"But I love you," Tom kept saying to me when I told him I wanted a divorce.

"It's not enough," I'd reply.

"But I bring home all my pay. I don't drink or run around. Why isn't it enough?"

"Because you are never home, never here for me."

We talked and talked. I didn't want to hurt him, but I was miserable. Finally, we decided to get away, take a weekend off, and settle the matter once and for all without six sets of little ears listening in.

On a Tuesday in November 1971, we hired a baby-sitter and headed south. We had no particular destination in mind. We'd just drive until we felt like stopping. We left Kentucky, drove through Tennessee, and into Alabama. About six o'clock, I pointed to a Cabana Hotel sign high above an entrance ramp near Birmingham. "Let's stop here," I said. "I can use a drink."

Agreeing that one hotel seemed as good as any other, Tom left the four-lane and pulled into the parking lot. *A lot of cars here,* I thought. *Hope they still have a room. If not, at least I can buy a drink.* While Tom went to the registration desk, I waited in the lobby. It was bustling, packed with people who were smiling and talking as though they all knew one another. Something about the scene made me feel uncomfortable. As I stood there watching, a large woman wearing a technicolored muumuu came toward me. I tried to step out of her path, but before I could stop her she had wrapped an arm around my shoulders and pulled me close. "Where y'all from, Sister?" she said in an Alabama drawl.

You've got the wrong number, I thought as I pulled away.

Not seeming to notice, she continued, "What's your name, honey?"

I don't know why I told her but I did. And she quickly wrote it down on a sticky-backed name tag that she brazenly posted on my blouse. On the tag was a silhouette of a bird. *A pigeon,* I thought. Oddly enough, the sight of that bird pleased me. It made me think of my dad back in Holland where carrier pigeons are a big sport. Every Sunday afternoon Dad would be up on the roof waiting for his pigeons to arrive home from whereever they had been sent.

Tom came up and gave a report. "We have a room." He glanced at my shoulder. "What's with the sign?"

How could I explain? "Tom, we've got to get out of here," I answered, rolling my eyes. "It's a pigeon convention and these people are too much."

"Look," he answered, "we're tired. We've driven a long way. They've got a room, let's just stay."

We went upstairs and changed our clothes for dinner; I put on a brown and white miniskirt. Then we squeezed into a down elevator crammed with women in long gowns and men in dark suits. It was packed so full we couldn't get near the panel to choose a floor-number. As the door opened on the second floor, we were swept out with the crowd and were hardly off the elevator when one of the conventioneers threw an arm across Tom's shoulders, and led him away with Tom gesturing to me helplessly.

More interested in finding a drink than in losing Tom, I followed the crowd to their destination. Taking the ballroom sign literally, I figured they were heading to a room for dancing where there'd surely be a bar.

Wrong. The ballroom was already teeming with people, not dancing, though many of them were swaying and waving their hands in the air. The room was set up as a lecture hall with row after row of lined chairs facing a stage and a lectern. A large, nonsensical banner hung across the back wall of the stage: FGBFI, it read.

I didn't see a bar, and yet, once in the room, there was no leaving for the crowd moved *en masse* toward the seats. Finally, I decided to follow the line of least resistance and sat down in a chair in the middle of a row, just as a handsome man carrying a leather-bound book came on to the stage.

I was horrified when I heard the first words out of his mouth: "Praise the Lord!" Straight from Texas, this guy didn't need amplification by any microphone.

He's a preacher! Get me out of here! I said to myself. But I waited, not wanting to make a show of myself by leaving so quickly. I listened to the man for a few minutes until I'd had enough. I stood up and was struggling my way through the row when I heard the man say something that stopped me cold. "There are unhappy people in this room, people who are here to get a divorce. They need to know that the Lord Jesus Christ can fix anything, if they'll just sit and listen."

I went back to my seat, sat down, and I listened. A half hour later, when the man was winding down, he looked out over the audience, raised a finger, and pointed straight at me. "If you let Jesus Christ into your life," he said, "He'll save your marriage."

Who does this man think he is, invading my life like that? I'll go up there and we'll just see about this Jesus saving my marriage. With an angry, daring spirit, I stepped into the aisle and walked to the foot of the stage.

Face to face with the preacher who'd stepped down from the platform, I said, "Okay, I want to meet this Jesus; where is He?"

"Sister," he said, "you ask Him to move into your heart and He will. Just ask Him in your own words."

What does "moving into my heart" mean? I had no idea. *Is this marriage a "till death do us part" commitment that will be troublesome to break?* Filled with those questions, I silently prayed, *Jesus, I want You to come in, but if I don't like You, can I ask You to leave?*

In response to my honest questions, a brilliant light appeared. The best way I can describe it is that it was like having a bright, flashing bulb inside me that burst with its radiance from my head to my feet and back—three times before it settled in somewhere near my heart. I began to feel a terrible itching in my left breast. I was embarrassed. I was sure everyone would be staring at my chest because of the glow it was giving off.

The preacher still stood in front of me. Now I spoke to him about what I was feeling. It was as though I were a child again and my words were the words of an innocent little girl. "I think He—Jesus—has moved in," I said, "but would you ask Him if He would turn off the light? It itches. It's too bright, and I don't like it there."

He smiled. "I don't know about that; I don't see any light, but Jesus says He is the Light—and the Truth and the Way."

Right then a little eighty-year-old lady tapped me on the shoulder. "Did you say it was itching?" she asked. "Here in Alabama we say that if something itches, it's healing. Honey, God's healing your heart."

When I turned around to talk with her, I saw Tom standing behind her. His toothy smile. His big brown eyes brimming with tears. In a second he was at my side. "I asked Jesus into my heart," I whispered.

"So did I," he said.

My heart still itching, I left the ballroom with Tom. At a table in the corridor, the tall man who'd swept Tom off the elevator convinced us to buy Bibles. Tom bought me a red King James Version; I bought him a brown one. "The Bible's your manual," the man said. "For your marriage. For your new Christian life."

"Well, what are the pigeons for?"

"Ma'am, they're not pigeons," he said, holding back a belly laugh. "They're doves and they represent the Holy Spirit. Read the Bible; start with the Gospel of John. It will tell you about the dove."

For the remainder of the time we were there Tom and I feverishly read "the manual"; we started with John and kept going. Despite the King James English and my general discomfort reading English (my second language) I understood the message. We went back to the ballroom for other meetings of what we learned was a convention for Full Gospel Businessmen's Fellowship International—FGBFI.

We returned home on Sunday never having discussed divorce. With the Lord's help, we put our marriage and family back together. "My kids" and "his kids" soon learned they were our kids.

Two years later we moved north. Tom traveled less; two years after that, in 1975, we had a child of our own.

But in May 1977, a month after my thirty-ninth birthday, our life—my life—fell apart. After three days of nausea and headache, I went to a doctor, who took my blood pressure, looked in my eyes, and sent me to a hospital. After giving me an angiogram, a neurologist stood over my bed and told Tom and me to gather in our children; with two aneurysms at the base of my brain, I wasn't expected to live more than forty-eight hours.

I was young enough and at this point strong enough that I challenged his prognosis. "You think you're God? Telling me how long I'll live. No way."

He left the room and got on the phone to call a neurological surgeon in Los Angeles, then another in Boston. The odds were too slim for my survival; no one would take my case.

Finally, after I'd survived ten days beyond my fated forty-eight hours, a doctor in London, Ontario, said yes. If I survived the ambulance ride, he'd operate.

But with every hour of pain I lost physical stamina and the will to live. Before being loaded into the ambulance, I told Tom it would be better if I just lay there and died. "I'll be better off in heaven, anyway," I reasoned. "I'm ready to go and maybe the doctor's right. If it's my time, it's my time. Let's just get it over with."

Tom wouldn't hear of it. "No," he said with quiet certainty. "God wants to do something here."

I did survive the day-long ride north across the border. And a marathon eight-hour operation. But the next day a clip slipped in at the base of my skull. The doctor wanted to operate again, this time for an estimated six hours of surgery.

Tom and I said okay, but in my heart I was ready to give up. As they wheeled me into the operating room, I prayed, *Lord, the Bible says "to die is gain." I want to gain. It's okay, just let me die.*

I'd said the words silently, but in response I heard a voice, a man's voice that seemed to come from my hair follicles, from my fingers, my toenails. "Anna," he said, "that's not the entire sentence."

I tried to keep the conversation going. "Yes, it is, Lord. I read it. Look it up Yourself; it's in the New Testament."

The next thing I knew a recovery-room nurse was slapping at my cheek, asking me what my name was. I didn't answer her question. I asked one of my own. "What's the other half of the sentence?"

Relieved that I was conscious, she went out and reported to Tom. "Anna's coming around okay. But she's talking gibberish, asking about 'the other half of the sentence.'"

Hoping to set me at ease, Tom had the presence of mind to say, "Ask Anna what the first half of the sentence is."

"To die is gain," I told her.

And she soon brought me Tom's answer, straight from Paul's epistle (Philippians 1:21, KJV). "Anna, the sentence begins 'to live is Christ.' Does that make sense to you?"

Under the fog of anesthesia, I put a negative twist on the line. *God doesn't want me!* I thought. *Why? What's wrong with me that I have to stay here?*

173

Ten days after surgery I was alive, but failing fast. My left side was completely immobile and the paralysis had affected my throat: I could breathe and manage a muffled talk, but I couldn't swallow, not even my saliva. I was so thin, about ninety-five pounds, and so pricked full of holes that my veins were collapsing and IVs were a problem. I was so weak I couldn't even raise my good arm off the mattress.

It may have been spring outside my hospital window, but in my spirit it was bleak midwinter. *I'd be better off dead than in this condition. God, what's this about "to die is gain"? I don't get it.*

That was my state in the middle of one night when I heard the same male voice that had spoken as I rolled into the operating room. "Anna, swallow." It was a firm but kind command.

Out loud I muttered an equally firm answer: "I can't."

"Anna, swallow."

Lord, You know I can't. I'm so weak. I'm paralyzed.

Like young Samuel in the Old Testament, I heard a third call in the night: "Anna, swallow."

I expect he meant for me simply to swallow my saliva, but with a fighting, even angry spirit, as if to prove that I was right and the voice was wrong, I tried to lift my right arm and reach for a glass of water an aide had placed on my bedside table. Could it be? In one grand swoop I grasped the glass, picked it up, and brought it to my lips.

When I heard that mouthful of heaven hit the bottom of my stomach, I let loose with a jubilant scream.

Immediately, for the first time since my surgery, I reached for the buzzer and called a nurse. A disbelieving doctor was soon at my side ordering someone to bring me Cream of Wheat. And when Tom arrived, I told him to find me a milkshake. I'd prove to him that I was on the mend.

And I was. Several weeks later Tom supported my weight as I feebly put one foot in front of the other, trying to walk toward the corporate jet his company had generously sent to take me home. As we inched our way across the runway, I nodded toward the company symbol, a glass blower, painted on the plane's tail. "Look, Tom. It's the angel Gabriel blowing his horn in praise."

After several more weeks of inpatient physical therapy and rehabilitation, I slowly walked up the stairs of my own airy, open, California-style house. Being July, the kids were home during the day, and I set up a command center in my upstairs bedroom. From the doorway I could look down to the first floor and across the hallways, a bridge spanning the living room like a loft.

Resting in bed one afternoon, praising God and reading the prophecies of Isaiah, I heard the bridge creak, a telltale sign that someone was looking for me. I looked up, expecting that Tom had forgotten something and come home from the office.

My visitor wasn't Tom at all. In the doorway I saw a giant dressed in white, linen-like, hooded and floor-length robe, a rope at his waist, long loose sleeves. Above the door frame the wall was invisible; his head reached to the ceiling—nine feet tall.

"Hello," he said. It was not the same voice I'd heard in the hospital. Walking into the room, he held out his hand.

"Hi." I didn't know him by name and had never seen him before, yet my spirit recognized him as a friend. It was clear that he wanted to clasp hands but he had no intention of taking my hand. I would have to reach out to his.

When I did, he said he wanted to show me something.

My hand in his, we left the bedroom, soaring up through the roof, through the sky as we mortals see it. We traveled so fast that the wind laid my short hair (maybe an inch long, having been shaved for my surgery) flat against my head. We kept going and at the top of what I'd call a second heaven, we stopped. Floating in the air, we turned around and looked down on planet Earth, a blue jewel in a sea of black. It was more awesome than photos taken by astronauts. The planet was clearly turning on its axis as it was spinning round.

"It's so beautiful." My vocabulary didn't seem adequate.

"Look again," the giant said.

Without any effort on my part, my eyes changed their focus, like lenses in a pair of binoculars. Suddenly, I saw a woman coming out of a grocery store, heading for her car in a crowded parking lot. I saw what she carried in her paper bag: bread, toilet paper, laundry soap. I didn't recognize the particular place and didn't ask. Again, it was hard for me to find words.

"Look again," he said.

I blinked my eyes and again they refocused to a new dimension. I gasped at what I was allowed to see and hear: Each blade of grass, each piece of wood furniture, each rock in a driveway or creekbed had a voice and was singing an otherworldy song of praise. The small stones sang softly; the large rocks sustained a louder volume. I saw trees: branches covered not with leaves but with hands clapping; their voices sang a joyful "praise the Lord." All in perfect harmony. At the seashore, as every wave hit the beach it said "Hallelu—jah," the "jah" one long whoosh.

"It's so beautiful. I'll never forget this," I said, tears rushing down my cheeks.

"See that you don't," the giant said firmly.

He then went on to explain the sights I'd seen. "God's creation naturally raises its voice to praise God. But humans, they have been given a will; they have a choice to praise or not. God is so pleased with praise that when humans praise Him, He tells creation to be still, because He is listening to Anna...or Tom...or..."

Was I in this second heaven for minutes—or hours? Again, I don't know. Still holding my hand, my white-robed friend flew me back to earth. He left as I felt my spirit entering my body. I had to make myself small to reenter my body, down through the top of my head.

There I sat, with my Bible open to the prophecy of Isaiah:

> *You will go out in joy*
> *and be led forth in peace;*
> *the mountains and hills*
> *will burst into song before you,*
> *and all the trees of the field*
> *will clap their hands.*

(Isaiah 55:12, NIV).

The mountains and hills singing praises! The trees clapping hands!

Yes! And the angel's message is confirmed again in the gospel, where Jesus Himself said, "I tell you...if [my disciples] keep quiet, the stones will cry out" (Luke 19:40, NIV).

The rest of the day is a blur in my memory. I'm sure the children were in and out of the house and my room, but my mind was preoccupied, mulling over the sights and sounds evident from the heights of the second heaven. Who would ever believe me? *Tom will think the surgery fried my brain*, I thought, and it was six weeks before I told him.

"See that you don't forget." It was the giant's one command for my life back on this solid sod.

Forget? How could I?

I could never forget in the springtime, when the river rushes its banks, when the dogwoods and daffodils burst open with praise to their Creator.

I could never forget in the summer, when the oaks in the yard shade us from the high sun, when I see every day the leaves that are hands clapping their joy.

I could never forget in the autumn, when the hillsides burn with fiery reds and yellows, when the vines banking the Finger Lakes hang heavy with their grapes.

It might be easy to forget in winter, when the naked branches and barren knolls bespeak abandonment and death, but I can't even forget then. For in the bleakest of my personal winters, my Creator was at work. In ways I didn't understand He was preparing my heart for His presence. And in ways I don't understand, He is working in the stark trees, which are not dead but alive and singing a happy song.

No matter what the season, I remember what I was shown about nature. And I also remember what I'd been told about humans: we have a choice of whether or not we praise.

And praise, I do.

Don't laugh. I sing my life-song even as I polish my oak furniture. If no one's home and I start vacuuming, I address the chairs and table. "Quiet. It's my turn," I say.

Then louder than the Hoover, I belt out the praises:

> *Be silent ye mountains, ye fields and ye*
> *fountains.*
> *For this is the time I must sing,*
> *It's the time to sing praises to the Rock of*
> *the Ages,*
> *And this is the time I must sing.*

～ Pam Kidd ～

TOWARD THE END OF "A SCENT OF FLOWERS," Pam Kidd mentions writing a
script about her experience with angels for a proposed television special. That
script was accepted and produced, and after the program was aired on the
Discovery Channel in April 1995, the letters flooded into the Kidd home in
Brentwood, Tennessee. "People from everywhere, from all walks of life,
wanted to tell me about their own dramatic encounters," Pam says. "Many of
them wrote that I had given them the courage to speak out for the first time.
They were relieved to find that other people had also had such visitations.
`Now I don't feel so alone,' more than one person confessed."

Later, Pam helped arrange an evening on the subject of angels at Hillsboro
Presbyterian Church in Nashville where her husband David is the pastor. It
was an ecumenical occasion in which many of the distinguished religious fig-

ures who had appeared on the television special, including a Catholic priest and a Jewish rabbi, spoke. The turnout was so large—another indication of the increased interest in angelic hosts—that other such interfaith programs are in the offing.

David Kidd has been pastor at Hillsboro since 1972, the same year that their son Brock was born. Once an agnostic, David had studied to be an anthropologist, until one evening nearing the completion of his Ph.D. at Brown University, he was sitting alone in his room when he had a spiritual conversion. With a sharp and immediate change in direction, he applied to three different divinity schools. The first to accept him was Vanderbilt University in Nashville, and that's how he went to Tennessee where he met and married a young woman from Chattanooga, Pam. The newlyweds spent two years as missionaries in the Appalachian Mountains, then David received a call to an old Nashville church that was making its last gasp for life after a move to the suburbs had depleted the bulk of its membership. Today, that church, Hillsboro, has been recalled to vigorous life; only recently, in a Boston-based publication, *Acting On Your Faith,* it was chosen as one of seventy churches and synagogues nationwide for a congregation "making a difference."

Writing about her angels is a form of witnessing, Pam Kidd feels. "My angels are a validation of God's reality. I want as many people as possible to know about them. And if they don't believe me when I tell about the experience, well, what can I say? It happened; it made everything better. For me it's like a valentine from a secret admirer. It says 'somebody loves you.'"

A Scent of Flowers

by Pam Kidd

"The Lord gave and the Lord has taken away;
may the name of the Lord be praised."

—Job 1:21 (NIV)

HEN HE DIED, MY FATHER WAS STILL A BOY AT HEART, and that boy belonged to my children, Keri and Brock. At age sixty-two, a year before his death, he broke his leg playing football with ten-year-old Brock. The doctor laughed and said the play had resulted in "the world's oldest football injury."

When we'd visit Chattanooga in the fall, he would go out in the yard, rake up the dogwood and redbud leaves into a big pile, and lead the "let's jump" parade, all six-foot-four of him running straight for the heap.

When we'd arrive he and the children would disappear for hours inside his workshop, a small room off the garage. There he would fix the treasures they'd brought for him to repair, a doll with a severed arm, a truck with a broken axle. They'd paint pictures on scraps of two-by-fours or hammer them together to make a boat. They'd talk about things kids talk about.

My children owned my father, as did I. From the day I was born, he and I had been best pals, even soulmates. Sometimes in the night I'd wake up and be afraid. I'd go to my parents' bedroom, stand inside the door, and listen for the rhythm of my father's breath. Then I'd match my breathing to his, in, out, measure for measure. After a while I'd feel tired, less tense. As if his strength had become mine, I could return to bed and sleep.

On Holy Thursday 1984 I volunteered a few hours in Keri's second-grade classroom and then brought her home. We were both anticipating the holiday weekend: On Good Friday my mother and father were driving from Chattanooga to Nashville to visit us.

But when I pulled in the driveway, my husband David stood waiting for me on the front stoop. "Pam, I'm sorry," he said. "Your father has had a heart attack."

"Then we need to go right away to be there."

"Pam, he's dead."

How did I respond to those words? I consciously inhaled—and wondered if I would be able to exhale. If Daddy had lost his breath, would I lose mine? I was actually surprised that the air emptied from my lungs. One breath, then two. I was alive!

While David got the family ready to travel, I walked out to the spring that flowed through the back of our property. *This is when I'm going to break down, lose control, maybe even my breath,* I thought. But in the sound of the flowing water I found a peace beyond my mortal understanding. I was breathing on my own. Alive! I had wonderful memories. I had no regrets. As for Daddy, he'd gone quickly, as he'd always hoped. He was with his Lord and smiling down on me with the love that would never leave his face.

Early evening we drove into my parents' driveway in Chattanooga. The cross-shaped dogwood blossoms hung like an umbrella over my father's manicured grass, blooming tulips, and trimmed rosebushes. Yet the red brick colonial house had a barren look: Daddy himself wasn't standing on the stoop, waving his hearty welcome.

Both Brock and Keri bounded out of the car. After hugs and hellos from their grandmother, whom we all called Bebe, they headed straight for Pa's workshop. I sensed a child's wild hopes that maybe, just maybe, they'd find him there. He'd be waiting for them. He'd be laughing that the story of his death had been a joke.

David and I joined my mother in the den, eager to rehash the details of the day. Away on an overnight business trip to Birmingham, Daddy had died alone in a hotel room while getting dressed for breakfast. His body would be sent back to Chattanooga, to arrive before morning.

Suddenly my mother grew agitated and yet very focused. "Are the kids in the shop?" she asked.

"Yes, Bebe," I answered, "they needed to see his room."

"Oh, David. Go there right now. There's a loaded gun on the second shelf, on the left. Ever since that robbery, Harrison has left it....Hurry. If Brock picks it up—" A month before, a thief had plundered their house, even their bedroom, while they slept. They'd installed a security system, but Daddy had apparently still been nervous.

David ran out of the room, my mother and I following behind. "I don't see it, Bebe," David said. "Pa must have put it away."

"No. It was right here," she said as she entered. She turned to the shelving on the left and placed her palm on the second shelf. "Right here."

Keri spoke up. "Here's what *I* found on that shelf. An Annie doll. Pa left it for me."

"But did you see a gun?" Bebe asked.

"No." Neither Keri nor Brock had seen a weapon, though they had obviously canvassed the room. The shelf was well above the children's heads, but they had climbed on the footstool looking for treasure. On that same shelf, Brock had found a pocket knife with his name—in Daddy's handwriting—on the box.

Before we left the room, we all searched, and we all agreed: no gun—toy or real, loaded or empty.

Even so, Bebe suggested the kids leave the shop. She shut the door behind us, and we returned to the den and the cares and carings that come with death: A neighbor stopped with a casserole. The phone rang. We made calls and plans. And finally, we went to sleep, exhausted.

While most people downsize when their children leave home, my parents had bought a larger house to make room for their grandchildren. The room I now considered "mine" had some of my childhood furnishings. But when I'd married, Bebe had replaced my twin beds with one black iron bed, big enough for two. And "my" first-floor bedroom had no windows. When you went to bed, closed the door, and turned the light off, the room was positively black.

I slept soundly until, deep in the night, I woke with a start. *Someone* was in the room, standing near the foot of the bed. I heard nothing except David's sleepy breath, and yet I knew an intruder was there. *The thief. He's returned.* The thought had hardly lodged in my mind when the scent of flowers came to my nostrils. I smelled a spring bouquet heavy with the sweetness of roses. Slowly, I turned toward David in the pitch dark. He hadn't stirred. As I leaned back toward the presence, the aroma wafted stronger and sweeter than before.

I lay there mystified, no longer fearful, yet still certain, absolutely certain, that someone was standing near the foot of my bed. And this someone was holding a huge bouquet of fragrant flowers. After what seemed five or ten minutes, the presence left, stealing the fragrance away.

Not wanting to wake David, who sleeps soundly and cannot go back to sleep if disturbed, I slipped out of bed and went upstairs to my mother's room.

"Bebe."

She answered immediately, as if she hadn't been sleeping.

"I woke up and knew there was someone in my room. A visitor. . . ." When I'd finished my story, she slipped on her robe. We two cased that house, room by room, up and down, looking and sniffing like police dogs. We even opened the door and turned on the light in the furnace room. Nothing was out of place. What's more, nothing smelled remotely like flowers.

Had the someone been Daddy? The thought crossed my mind, but I wasn't convinced. "Bebe, in the summertime, remember, Daddy would get up early and cut a rose in the garden? He'd sneak in my room and put it in the vase on my bedside table. When I woke up it was there, still wet with the dew."

She smiled. He did love his flowers. Leaving on his Wednesday trip, his last words to her had been "I love you," as he handed her a big bunch of tulips.

Finally we detectives dropped our fruitless investigation and went back to bed, drawing no real conclusions except that everything seemed perfectly under control.

The next morning my brother arrived, and we went to the funeral home. The memory of the unseen presence and the gift of fragrance bolstered the peace I'd first felt sitting by the spring in my own backyard.

I've said my father belonged to his grandchildren. That was obvious on Friday when Brock and Keri and my brother's daughters first saw their pa laid out in the casket. Horrified at the obvious makeup on his face, they rubbed it off with their fingers. They asked for a comb so they could make his hair look right. With his new penknife Brock cut dogwood branches, and the girls ringed the inside of the casket with the pink and white blossoms. They put love notes and snapshots in Pa's chest pocket, and Brock propped in the casket a large photo of him and Pa speeding down a hill on a wooden sled.

Hundreds of people came to pay their respects to Daddy. They walked into the parlor downcast, grieving that death would take such a young, fine man. One after another they'd walk up to the casket and then burst into smiles. They knew Daddy's spirit. It was easy to imagine how he would have responded to his grandchildren's loving gestures. He would have thrown back his head and laughed the magnificent, booming laugh that came so easily to him.

A year later, we drove home to Bebe's when the springtime flowers were in luscious bloom. The dogwood crosses formed a canopy over her backyard. As usual, we all went into Daddy's shop to reminisce awhile. In that room we most keenly felt his presence; it's where he'd left his clearest mark.

Bebe and I sat down in the hard-back chairs, and she brought up a subject she'd mentioned repeatedly in the last year: Daddy's gun. The loaded 9-mm pistol that she'd never unearthed, though she had torn the shop apart—in an old-fashioned, housecleaning manner—looking for it.

Bebe turned to David, leaning against the shelf where Keri had found her Annie doll the night Pa died. "You know, David, I never did find that gun," she said.

Without comprehending what he might be saying, David answered, "You mean this gun?"

Bebe nearly lost her senses. There inside its unzipped case lay Dad's pistol. A yellow note was stuck to the outside of the wrapper. In big black letters, unmistakably Daddy's scrawl, the note said, "Do not touch. Loaded." And indeed it was.

"*Nobody* has been in this room," Bebe assured us—and herself. "We have the security system…. I cleaned every inch of this room myself, including that shelf. You all were *here* when we looked for it last spring. Now it appears, exactly where Harrison left it. What's going on?"

Of course, this side of heaven I'll never *know* who brought me a floral bouquet the night of Daddy's death. And the gun? I kept wondering, *What was going on?* My husband did not sneak that gun onto the shelf. Bebe is a good housekeeper, and she did not dust around the weapon.

For two more years these mysteries puzzled me. Then, on a 1987 vacation in Mexico, I received a clue from an elderly tour guide showing us an ornate angel statue in a historic church in Mexico City. His lecture included information about the art but also about angels themselves. One line caught my attention: "When angels visit the earth, they sometimes announce their presence with the scent of flowers, especially roses."

When angels visit...especially roses! I couldn't get the thought out of my mind.

Back home, I read everything about angels I could get my hands on. If you go looking for angelic accounts, you do see a pattern; over and over I read descriptions of the sweet smell of flowers.

I choose to believe that God sent two angels the day Pa died. One to give blessing: flowers in the night to soothe my soul. And one to take away danger: the gun my father had left out, not knowing my children might come bounding into his shop in his absence.

In a difficult time of personal loss, the biblical Job had the grace to say,

> *The Lord gave and the Lord has taken away;*
> *may the name of the Lord be praised*
> (Job 1:21, NIV).

When I think of my father—his breath and his death—I whisper Job's prayer of praise.

When I think of the angels guarding my family—well, sometimes David and the kids roll their eyes. They think I've become an angel fanatic. It's probably best that they don't know that when I'm going some place alone, I clear the front passenger seat of the car—to remind myself that my angel is there. While driving I talk to her.

Brock has just graduated from the University of Tennessee in Knoxville, and Keri from high school. But when they were still at home and walking out my door to get on a school bus, I'd say good-bye and then imagine an angel getting on that bus with them.

I've never *seen* their angels, but I know they're there. I imagine Keri's guardian angel as being a big white swan, always hovering over her, ready to enfold and protect her. Brock? Knowing the gusto he brings to life, I picture him having two angels; they're big, burly, very muscular, and dressed in armor. Sometimes I imagine them lying on his car, like two gigantic hood ornaments, ready to lead him through the night.

After graduation Brock left for a trip to Europe. People who know I've been a careful, cautious mother ask me if I'm worried about him, so far away, among strangers in every sense of the word.

No. I know his angels got on the plane with him. "Brock," I said, "everywhere in Europe you're going to see angels. Statues in fountains. Carvings on cathedrals. Paintings in galleries. You can't miss them in the Old Country art. And every time you see one, I want you to remember that they're following you. They are. And if you need any help, call on them."

"Oh, Mom." You can imagine the exasperated college-kid response.

But asking for help works. It worked dramatically the night several years ago when the radio was warning of flash floods in our area. The rain was torrential. We knew what flash floods could mean. Once before, the stream at the edge of our property had become a raging river, tearing down fences and washing away a seven-hundred-pound pool filter in our back yard.

O Lord, not again! Please! We simply couldn't afford another round of repairs. And the physical labor of the cleanup was unthinkable. Nearly hysterical, I stomped out into the rain and mud— wearing high heels—and asked God to post angels around our pool. "I want an angel here! And here! And here!" I shouted every six paces. "I don't want this pool to flood, because I can't handle it right now. God, please, hold back the water."

We tied down what we could and went to bed. Still praying. Still hoping. With the morning light we discovered that the water had risen to within three inches of the pool.

That day I picked soaked branches and dead fish out of the yard—every inch of it mud—singing praises of thanksgiving for the angels posting guard.

I believe God dispatches messengers to change our lives. Angels have even changed the course of my career. It started the day after our backyard flooded. Overflowing with thanksgiving, I hunted down a phone number for Peter Shockey, a Nashville filmmaker who produced *Life after Life*, an amazing film we'd seen about after-death experiences. I got him on the line. I don't advise anyone to take this route to a professional relationship, but I said, "I know you're going to think I'm crazy, but I'm a writer and…if you're working on another project, I'll write for free, because I owe the angels a favor."

Well, we did work together. For no fee I wrote him a grant proposal for a TV film about angels. When the Discovery Channel funded the production, Peter hired me to write the script—this time for pay.

For now, that project consumes my days. It excites me because one of the most important things that comes with believing in angels is sharing the news with other people. The Discovery Channel film offered an unbelievable opportunity to spread the word: In life or death, we are not alone! God loves us enough to give us guardians, whether we see them or not.

"May the name of the Lord be praised."

May Jesus Christ, the king of glory, help us to make the right use of all the myrrh that God sends, and to offer to him the true incense of our hearts; for his name's sake, Amen.

—Johann Tauler

Anna Penner & Helen Grace Lescheid

OVER HALF A CENTURY AGO, Anna Penner and her grandniece, Helen Grace Lescheid, lived in little Ukrainian villages no more than twenty kilometers from each other. These were Mennonite communities and the people there were mostly German, the descendants of settlers to whom Catherine the Great had offered religious and ethnic freedom if they would come and cultivate the steppes. In time grand orchards and wheat fields appeared.

Today, long after the upheavals and torments of World War II, the two women are neighbors again, both residents of Abbotsford, British Columbia, where Anna has lived since her arrival there in 1955. Helen Grace is a registered nurse and a writer. They may have been transplanted from another continent and another time, but one important element remains the same for each of them: their Mennonite faith.

For many years Anna was a cook in a home for seniors, but she is in her nineties now, content to live quietly in the house she shares with Helen Grace's mother. One day while Helen Grace was paying a visit, she and her great-aunt were chatting casually, when Anna began to tremble.

"I was remembering something from the war," she explained in the German language of her birth, for she does not speak English. Then, through her tears, as though she was delivering of herself a great burden, out came in vivid detail the memory she had kept hidden for fear of being thought *seltsam* (queer) if she told it to anyone. *"Das ist wirklich passiert! Das ist wirklich passiert!"* she kept saying about a mystifying light that had come to her. "It really happened! It really happened!"

Tante Anna (as Helen Grace calls her) had a stroke in April 1995. Strong-willed as ever, she was not long in getting herself about the house and doing some cooking. Even at her great age, just before her stroke she would set out to walk three blocks to church alone on a dark winter night.

"Aren't you afraid?" people would ask.

"Afraid? Why should I be?"

If friends looked at her quizzically, she just smiled and thought again about the night when fear evaporated forever through the miracle of a heavenly light—the light that her grandniece has carefully recorded here.

Lead, Kindly Light

by Anna Penner
as told to and translated by Helen Grace Lescheid

Lead, kindly Light, amid the encircling gloom,
Lead thou me on;
The night is dark, and I am far from home,
Lead thou me on.
Keep thou my feet: I do not ask to see
The distant scene: one step enough for me…

So long thy power hath blest me, sure it still
Will lead me on,
O'er moor and fen, o'er crag and torrent, till
The night is gone.
And with the morn those angel faces smile
Which I have loved long since, and lost awhile.

—John Henry Newman

THOUGH MY FAMILY WAS GERMAN, I grew up in Ukraine, along the western shore of the mighty Dnieper River, with its white sandy beaches. We were a close Mennonite community in the village of Nieder Chortitza; on summer evenings we'd gather in the shade of an orchard to play games and sing German folk songs. I'd strum a guitar and join my strong soprano voice to the harmonizing altos, tenors, and basses. As a child I didn't imagine the twists and turns my life path would take.

In 1922, during my twenty-second year, our wonderful Ukraine lost its independence to Russia, becoming part of the U.S.S.R. In time, the Communists, led by Stalin, took away our farms and most of the produce we harvested on the communal farms. To survive we snared gophers and hunted roots and edible leaves.

The Communists closed our churches and exiled many families and young people to Siberia. Under cover of darkness, a small group of Mennonite believers left their homes and gathered at a designated place to worship. "It's God's will to praise Him, Anna," my widowed mother would say, urging me to join her at the secret meetings. "And I'm going to praise Him as long as I can."

The only child still living at home, I felt protective of Mother; I didn't want her going alone. We'd pull kerchiefs over our faces and hurry off to a granary. In a dark cobwebby corner, I'd sit on a sack of wheat and softly sing a hymn. I'd listen to Scripture reading and prayers that bolstered my young faith.

And yet I always kept one ear cocked to the door. At the slightest noise my heart would pound with fear. I'd clasp clammy hands together, mumbling, "Please, God, protect us." Parents had been banned to Siberia for praying with their children at mealtimes or observing a Christian holiday. What would they do to us? To me? Being young and strong, surely I'd be torn from my family and....

And then World War II broke out. We anxiously listened to our shortwave radio. With heavy hearts we could only imagine the distant grief, never dreaming how quickly it would strike us. With lightning speed in June 1941, German bombers flew over our village and dropped their deadly cargo east of the river. German tanks rolled into the village. Quickly Stalin's army blew up the bridge and dam, flooding the village.

Despite our precarious position—caught in the crossfire between the Germans and the Russians—during the war my widowed sister Neta, her two daughters and one toddler grandson came to live with us. We were a household of women. My sister's three grown sons had been banished to Siberia. My niece's husband had been drafted by the Russians. I had never married.

Incessant shelling kept us awake at night and indoors during the day. Neighbors and friends hitched up their wagons and left. But we had no wagons or horses and fleeing on foot was out of the question considering Mother's congestive heart failure. So we stayed and cowered in our small mud-brick house. When a corner of our house was hit, Neta and I quickly propped up some boards to keep the roof from caving in altogether.

Through this horror Mother's composure amazed me. "Children, I may not survive this war," she'd say softly. "But you are young and strong, and with God's help you may find a way to escape." Her face, furrowed by pains she seldom talked about, had the radiance of a person who has come to depend on God for safety. "I'm not afraid to die," she'd continue. "But I do want to have a decent burial. Anna, will you promise me that? A good Christian burial."

I'd grasp her fragile hand. "Of course, Mother. But you're not going to die. Not yet." I could only hope and pray that God would spare and protect us.

And it seemed our way of escape came in September 1943, when the retreating German army talked of evacuating our village. After all, most of us were German by ancestry; they wanted to help us. In hopes of a better future in Germany—at least peace and safety—we butchered our pig and made sausages; we cooked our chickens and roasted buns. I packed a small trunk with our most cherished possessions: my hymn book; books of poetry; a few paintings; a photo album. Neta stuffed bedding and clothes into a sack. My nieces packed a few belongings.

On October 5, an already-crowded army truck picked us up and delivered us to the train station. On the platform we huddled, as bombers screeched overhead. Russian or German? We couldn't tell. If only we could get away before another attack. Finally a German-run freight train rolled into town, and 163 of us—mostly women and children—crammed ourselves into the wooden boxcars until there wasn't room for more than a few people to sit at one time.

When the soldiers bolted the doors from the outside, we stood in darkness, the only available light seeping in through the cracks of the walls. For several days we Penner women hovered over Mother, whispering hope and assurances that life would be better at the end of the line.

Too often we heard the scream and roar of mortars and grenade explosions. To keep up courage and to pass the time, we'd sing folk songs and hymns, reminders of who we were and who our God was. Or I'd recite poetry. I had a favorite: *"Gott ist wo die Sonne glueht, Gott ist wo das Veilchen blüht...Ist kein Freund, kein Mensch bei Dir, Fürchte nicht, Dein Gott ist hier."* The poem's message is clear: "Don't be afraid. God is here."

At last we were allowed off the train. We lined up at a Red Cross truck distributing bread and coffee. We got milk for my young grandnephew and for Mother, whose heart was losing its grip. Her legs were swelling. She gritted her teeth against angina pain.

The next day the doors opened again, and we were ordered off the train. *This isn't the safety we were promised*, I moaned, as we refugees stepped toward the light—and the blast of machine guns and grenade explosions. A panicked German soldier shouted, "Out. Out. We're surrounded by Russians."

Grabbing Mother's arm, I pushed forward, following the surge of humanity driven by fear. It's bad enough being threatened by bullets and bombs when you're on familiar ground. The fear intensifies when you're displaced, in a strange place, refugees. "We've got to stick together," I said to Neta. "Let's find out where we are."

When I found out we were in Sereowka, a small town on the Ukrainian steppes, I wanted to cry. With frequent stops to repair rails and bridges, we hadn't actually progressed very far. Peace and freedom seemed like an elusive dream. Would we ever get there?

The Germans had vacated a few houses near the train station to accommodate us. In our temporary home, each night I slept beside Mother's bed; she would moan in pain. Her calves were swollen like elephant legs. And the angina crushed her chest. We hadn't been in Sereowka long when, in the middle of one night, I heard Mother mumble something. Raising myself on an elbow, I strained to hear her weak whisper.

"Would you like a drink, Mother?" I guessed.

"No. I don't want—anything," she gasped.

"What were you saying, then?"

"I was praying—for my children." She could hardly get the words out. "Anna, go to sleep. You are tired."

I pulled Mother's coat up around her and then rested my head back on my suitcase-pillow. I slept fitfully, so conscious of her pain, wishing fervently I could think of something to ease it. But what could I do?

Before dawn her moaning ceased. *Finally, she's gone to sleep,* I thought. I opened my eyes and looked into her face, *So peaceful....Too peaceful....She's not breathing....*

"Neta, Neta, wake up!" In seconds I had roused the whole family, and they wailed with me in grief. Even though I was still surrounded by loved ones, I felt so alone in the dark. Alone and afraid.

We hurriedly called together friends and former neighbors. A choir sang some of Mother's favorite hymns. A pastor read Scripture and prayed at the graveside. One comforting thought sustained me: *Mother, you've got your wish—a proper funeral. God is good. We couldn't have managed this if you'd died while we were travel-ing.* I tried not to think about the few children who'd died on the train; they'd been left in a potato field for some farmer or wild animal to find.

Two weeks after we laid Mother's weary body to rest, the Germans broke through the Russian barricade. We hurried back to the train station. We carried everything we could. Our trunk with its valuable contents stayed behind. But what did it matter? We'd escaped with our lives: we were moving west, toward safety.

Surviving a train collision that killed dozens, including children from our own village, we huddled through the winter on a freight train and then lived for several months in Dresden, where we lived in a school and worked in a factory. Then, with the Russians gaining ground, we were evacuated again. In March 1944 our train rolled into the station in Ratkersburg, a small Alpine town in German-occupied Yugoslavia.

To accommodate us, the Germans displaced the local villagers and gave their homes to us refugees. Some friends from Nieder Chortitza and I were placed in a house high up in the Alps, about ten kilometers from Ratkersburg. Neta and her daughters lived about five kilometers away.

Naturally, the local people resented, even despised, us. As we'd feared the Soviet communists back home, we now lived in fear of partisan activity against us. Wild stories circulated. Local partisans wearing firemen badges had raped refugee women, plundered their homes, shot at young people. Living in fear, we kept our doors bolted. Women never traveled alone. Our young people kept a strict curfew.

By December 1944 the battlefront was once again too close for comfort. Searchlights fanned the night skies. Explosions rocked the windows as Russian bombs hit or missed their targets. Once more our whole community feared for our lives and thought about evacuation.

I received a letter from my sister Tina, who had fled to Germany. "Come to Germany," she wrote. "You'll be safer here."

Yes, I'll go. It's time to leave. So three weeks before Christmas, a friend named Anna and I hopped the milk truck down the mountain to town. We took a train to Graz, Austria, to apply for a visa to move to Germany.

It was toward evening before we started home. As the dark settled in, it started to rain. Anna fidgeted in her seat. "Miserable night to be out walking," she muttered.

I agreed.

She thought for a minute and then announced, "I'm going to get off before Ratkersburg and spend the night at my son's. You're welcome to come with me, Anna."

No. It didn't feel right. I didn't want to worry my housemates needlessly by changing my plans and not coming home.

The train slowed and my friend picked up her purse. "Coming?" she asked hopefully.

"Thank you, but I need to go home."

Once she'd waved good-bye and disappeared into the dusk and descending fog, I sat there alone, suddenly desolate and gripped by fear. As we passed through the next village, I pressed my face to the cold window. I could barely make out the rooftops. The rain turned to sleet, pecking at the window pane. *Anna, I should have gone with you,* I thought, as if I were a child separated from my mother and wishing her back to my side. *If only I weren't alone in the dark....*

About eight o'clock, I stepped off the train in Ratkersburg. Since morning an icy wind had come up and it tore through my threadbare coat. My thin kerchief seemed useless. The sleet stung my face. Seeking out the shelter of the dimly lit train station, I sat on a bench and deliberated about the walk ahead of me: at least an hour uphill, on a black, starless night. The footpath lay between a cemetery and vineyards and dense forest—and I'd have to ford a rushing stream.

As I thought about the dangers, a panic flooded my being much as the Dnieper had flooded Nieder Chortitza. In the last twenty years, I'd braced myself for dangers and journeys. But tonight my courage failed me. Utterly alone, far from home in a foreign land, the dam broke. *No way!* I thought. *There's no way I can make that trip tonight. In the pitch dark. In this weather.*

The train had pulled out, the last train of the night. I looked around the lonely station and timidly approached the stationmaster. "Sir, could I spend the night here, please?"

"No, Ma'am," he said emphatically.

"I have so far to walk...."

"Ma'am, I can't allow it," he said abruptly. He grabbed his coat and hat and fished for keys in his pocket. Then he headed for the door.

The panic mired my feet. *I can't go up that mountain.*

At the door the stationmaster grew downright impatient. "C'mon. I'm locking this place up." He must have read the alarm in my eyes. More kindly he added, "During an air raid, you'll be safer up the mountain anyway."

It seemed a small comfort. I listened to the receding crunch of his boots on gravel; the only man who could have helped me vanished into the icy mist.

For a few moments I stood under the eaves of the straw roof. Finally I turned to the heavens, to the One my mother had turned to so often. "Father," I whispered, "I'm so scared. Take away this terror. Walk with me."

Suddenly there came a light, whiter than white and shining. It surrounded me.

Oh no, the bombers!

I scanned the sky for the telltale flares that preceded an air raid. I waited for the roar of planes, for the explosion of the hit.

Nothing. The sky was empty. Yet all around me the light shone. I felt as though I were standing in a dome, a huge globe of light about six feet across. Inside, it was bright as day. Outside, the night was black and strangely silent.

An indescribable peace suddenly filled my heart. I knew I could head toward the mountain. *I'll start out walking*, I thought with a robust confidence that I didn't have to force. With each step, the light moved with me, shining the path at my feet.

Instead of panic, joyous hymns welled up: "Oh, take my hand, my Father," I hummed softly, thinking it wise to stifle my strong urge to belt out the tune with my lusty soprano.

As I started my ascent, the wind stopped, then the sleet. In fact, it grew warm as a summer's night. I loosed my kerchief. *How strange to be so warm in December.*

When I reached the dangerous stream, the water glistened like a thousand diamonds. I clearly saw the series of flat rocks scattered across the foaming water. Surefooted, I stepped from one to the next to the next until I reached the far bank.

The light guided and cheered me all the way up the mountain. As I neared the old house, I looked back over the treacherous pass. Like a ribbon of light, it lay behind me. Excitedly I knocked on the door, wanting to show my friends the awesome sight. The door opened. A strong gust of wind grabbed it, almost tearing it off its hinges. "Anna! Come in!" my friend yelled, pulling me inside. My housemates crowded around me. "Such a dreadful storm! Weren't you afraid?" one asked.

"No," I shook my head. "The storm died...."

But I got no further. I suddenly could hear it too: the howling wind; the sleet pelting the windows; the moaning of the house.

While one friend busied herself with my supper, another took my coat. "It's dry," she said. Not quite believing what she was seeing, she repeated, "Anna, your coat's dry."

"I know," I said matter-of-factly.

I did my best to explain, but my friends looked at me with that puzzled expression I've come to expect. You see, from that night on I haven't known real fear, even in the succeeding months and years, when the pandemonium of the war—and the cold war—separated me from my family.

For months I lived in a refugee camp in Munich, Germany. Then I went to Paraguay for nine years before coming to British Columbia in 1955. I was reunited with my three sisters, nieces, and grandnieces—all had emigrated to western Canada.

In Paraguay I worked side by side with German Mennonite men, hacking out a place for our people in the dense jungle. Well into middle age, I carried buckets of damp earth away from a well-digging site. I cooked meals over primitive fires, feeding the men who built our houses. Eventually I owned a small hut with a straw roof—a home of my own. I lived alone, and at first I had no glass or wire netting to cover the windows, no lumber to build a proper door.

At times people warned me of thieves in the night or of poisonous snakes that would slither into open houses. Before December 1944, I would have been terrified. But no more. If fear drew near in the evenings, I'd start to sing, maybe "Oh, take my hand, my Father." Or I'd recite the poem I'd learned as a child: "Don't be afraid. God is here."

Don't be afraid. For fifty years it has been a theme of my life.

Don't be afraid. By the illuminating warmth of a kindly angelic light in wartorn Europe, it was God's word to me, a forty-year-old woman alone, afraid of the night.

Lighten our darkness, Lord, we pray; and in your mercy defend us from all perils and dangers of this night; for the love of your only Son, our Savior Jesus Christ.

—Evening prayer, from the ancient Gelasian Sacramentary

PART FOUR

Angels
Watching . . .
At Night

I have been young, and now am old;

yet have I not seen the righteous forsaken,

nor his seed begging bread.

He is ever merciful, and lendeth;

and his seed is blessed.

Psalm 37:25-26 (KJV)

Eileen Adair

EILEEN ADAIR HAS ALWAYS HAD A THIRST FOR TRAVEL. "I was born with itchy feet," she says. "I'm constantly curious about what lies around the next bend in the road." Eileen believes that all her life God has been setting up His direction signals for her, "but too often," she wrote recently, "I've been too thick-headed to recognize that it was He Who was calling the shots." One question that she answers for herself now is: "Does God really send His angels, as it says in Exodus 23:20 (NIV),'to bring you to the place I have prepared'?"

The first time that Eileen had reason to wonder about God's angels she was seventeen and her mother had been diagnosed with lung cancer. Within a week, she lay on her deathbed. "It was like something out of the movies," Eileen recalls. Her mother turned to her as she knelt on one side of the bed. She said her farewells. Then she turned to her husband on the other side.

"Daddy, I love you," she whispered.

"And I love you, honey," he answered.

With that, Eileen's mother laid her head back on the pillow. At that precise moment the parish priest knocked at the front door. "I was in the neighborhood," he told them, "and felt a very strong pull to come by and see how Mrs. Lynch was feeling."

The pastor administered last rites. As he said the prayers, the mother's eyes focused on a point where the ceiling joined the wall. "I was so struck with the expression on her face," Eileen remembers. "Her eyes sparkled and she smiled. She went to meet someone she recognized and was glad to see."

An angel? Jesus? Even then, as a teenager, Eileen knew that her mother had been met and ushered to a new home. She has a similar feeling today. In fact, she is convinced that where she lives now is a place she has been directed to, a place "prepared" for her.

Beaverton, Oregon, just outside Portland, is far from where her children and grandchildren live in Arizona, but it is where she feels at home. Her life is good. Recently retired from long years of work as a personnel assistant at Bonneville Power, a large electrical supplier in Portland, Eileen now does most of her itchy-foot traveling with a rock and gem club. The members hit the road in caravans, talking to one another over CB's as they drive to digs in search of sapphires in Montana, opals in Idaho, dinosaur bones in Utah, petrified wood in Oregon. Eileen likes to be in open country and the club provides a wonderful opportunity for a single woman to get there safely, and with interesting friends. She also belongs to a senior center where she has joined a weight-lifting program ("Your bones lose density as you get older. I don't envision giving up to age until I have to").

The one activity that brings Eileen the greatest satisfaction these days is her volunteer work at Vista House, an aerie 733 feet above the Columbia River

Gorge where people come from all over the world for the spectacular views. Eileen has developed a keen interest in the Columbia River itself. For a traveling woman who believes her life is firmly held in divine hands, the river has taken on a spiritual significance. She can talk poetically about the Columbia's "humble beginnings" in Canada, and how "this easily straddled stream" swells inexorably into a mighty force whose dams provide the electricity and lights and power for the entire Northwest. "I liken it to the power of God," she says, "and I am in awe."

Road Signs

by Eileen Adair

*"See, I am sending an angel ahead of you to guard you along the way
and to bring you to the place I have prepared.
Pay attention to him and listen to what he says...."*

—Exodus 23:20-21 (NIV)

Y GRANDDAUGHTER VANESSA recently came to visit me from Arizona. She's only eleven, too young to be contemplating major life decisions. But as someone who has lived a long time, I wanted to give her some advice I hope she'll never forget. After a conversation about the challenges of adolescence, I said, "When you have to make a decision, be still and listen to the quiet voice inside that says 'Turn this way' or 'Stay away from that.' Pay attention to God's messages." You see, I've learned that those messages are directions for the journey of life.

In my travels, I'm never as interested in my destination as much as the landscape that's between here and there. Out in the wide open spaces I see the grandeur of God; my faith breathes new life. If I were young today, I'd consider a career as a long-distance truck driver.

But that's not what young ladies did after the end of World War II. Trained as a secretary in April 1948, when I was twenty-one years old, I did the next best thing. I set out from home on my first solo, cross-country adventure. In Greensboro, North Carolina, I boarded a Greyhound bus and rolled west to visit a girlfriend who'd moved to Pasadena, California.

Let's just say I didn't take the direct route. I saw the country—Louisville, Chicago, St. Louis, Denver, Salt Lake City, Seattle, Victoria in British Columbia, San Francisco. Just when my friend in Pasadena thought I'd be arriving at her door, she'd receive another postcard, from another city. Early in June, I finally got there.

Low on cash, I found a job and stayed in California awhile...a long while. Twenty-eight years. In 1950, I met a handsome, utterly charming man. I chose to ignore the niggling voice inside ("Beware, this isn't right"), and he and I were married. Almost from the beginning I knew something was wrong. I was headed into a nightmare of a marriage.

But marriage is forever, I believed. I'd made a spiritual commitment. And so I stayed, and I raised two children as a stay-at-home mom. When I thought I couldn't endure another day of his insane tirades, I clung to my faith, which was fortified in the middle of one dark night. Wide awake, staring at the ceiling, I silently cried out for God to help me.

In response I heard a deep, commanding but gentle voice; it came from the corner of my bedroom. "Be still and know that I am God."

I waited and listened for more. Silence. I sat up to see who was there. No one.

When I lay back on the pillow, I fell into an uncommonly peaceful sleep. I did not then recognize the command as a verse from the Psalms, but the words became a part of me. And they took on new significance in the late seventies, when we moved from California to the desert sands of Arizona.

If I would just agree to move to Tucson, my husband assured me, we could make a fresh start. Life would be better. He promised. We sold our house and moved into a Tucson mobile home park, "temporarily," until we found the right property on which we would build. But one Friday night, eight months later, my husband phoned to say he wasn't coming home again—ever. Then on Monday I went to the bank to discover the surprise of my life: My cupboard was bare, our joint accounts empty. He had left and taken everything he could with him.

At an age when most people start to dream about retirement plans, here I was, no money, no job, a gas-guzzling '63 Chevy Bel Air station wagon, and two young-adult children not quite free from the nest.

My grown children, Michael and Valerie, rallied around and we focused on survival. I saw the mountains on either side of our mobile home as sentries sending me silent messages. They stood solid and strong, as I quavered, fragile and weak, convinced I would never again know joy. Out the kitchen window I watched the sun rise over the Rincon Mountains. The morning message was "I make all things new" (Revelation 21:5, KJV). At night I'd stand at the living room window as the sun set behind the majestic Tucson Mountains. As the day died I tried to hold on to the evening message: "Be still and know that I am God."

My children and I fell into a new routine. Michael and Valerie juggled part-time jobs and college courses. I took a clerk-typist job at the local Veterans' Administration Hospital. Over the next four and a half years, I moved several notches up the federal pay scale. But life was still a struggle, with not a dollar to spare at the end of the month. In time, Valerie married and temporarily moved to Florida. My son lived with me but had a steady job.

At the hospital I vigilantly read the job postings, hoping for higher-level positions—"upgrades," in governmentese. It never worked. Four times I applied for transfers and four times someone else was hired. Being determined, I set my sights on yet another VA job, in the Social Work Services Department. It offered higher pay and something important to me: more interaction with people.

That was my situation one night in November 1979, when Steve, a young man who'd grown up with my children in California, called from Portland, Oregon, where he'd moved with his parents, good friends of mine. "I just want you to know, Eileen, that you'll be here in Portland on November 23." It wasn't a question. It was a statement of fact. "That's the day I'm getting married," he continued.

"Oh, yeah, sure," I laughed. "And just where would I get the money to pull off a trip like that?" I asked.

"I'll tell you how you're gonna 'pull it off,'" he countered. "I've just bought you a round-trip plane ticket, because I want you here at my wedding, and I'm not going to take any excuses."

And there I was, enjoying the festive day and staying over with his mother, Marcella, through the next week.

Come Tuesday, Marcella asked me to ride along as she went downtown. "And while we're there, we'll have lunch," she said. "A nice little South Seas place I think you'll like."

She was right; the restaurant's food and atmosphere were memorable, but after lunch Marcella had another destination in mind. "We're real close to the federal building, Eileen. I thought we might stop by. Just for fun, let's go job shopping. Read the listings. See if they have any openings."

She was obviously talking about openings for me, and I didn't like the idea one bit. "They won't have anything secretarial," I said. "Even if they did, I'm not interested. I'm really sure I'll get that social work services upgrade in Tucson."

"Oh, come on. It'll be fun. It's just a game."

"Okay," I acquiesced, as she parked the car in the garage across the street from the eleven-story, sand-colored federal building. My mother had taught me something about being a cooperative houseguest. And, after all, Marcella *had* paid for my lunch.

We walked through the automatic doors into a sleek, spacious lobby. To our left I saw a "Job Information Center" sign. Marcella strode confidently toward the "technical and administration" postings.

Standing side by side, Marcella scanned one row of listings as I scanned another; I quickly had my answer. "No. There aren't any secretarial jobs listed at all. I told you. I guess we can leave now."

From all the way across the room, a clerk overheard my comment and offered a piece of unsolicited advice: "Looking for a secretarial position? I have some books you might be interested in looking through."

"Yes, and thank you." Marcella grinned, again taking the lead. To see the books, I had to fill out an "interest card," which I held in one hand as I flipped through a fat three-ring binder, each plastic-coated page listing one job.

To please Marcella, I mentioned the only vacancy that caught my attention: one grade above the job I was applying for in Tucson. "Something like this sounds like it might be interesting." The job was secretary to the area manager of the Office of Personnel Management, OPM.

The clerk was all ears and eager to please: "That job's right here in our office."

"Well," I told the clerk, "here's my interest card. You could just turn it in for me." Sure I'd satisfied my obligation to Marcella, I thought we were out the door.

"Usually, I could do that," the clerk answered, "but because the job is here at OPM, you have to take the card yourself, up to the third floor. Sorry."

Okay, what can it hurt to walk to the third floor?

But once there, the whole situation got out of control. A woman behind a desk took my card and picked up the phone. I looked at Marcella. "What's she doing?" I whispered.

"Just see what happens," she said under her breath.

Within seconds, an interviewer came out from a bank of offices and invited me down the hallway to a conference room. Maybe fifteen minutes later the no-nonsense questioner excused herself, left the room, and then returned. "The manager would like to meet with you. If you could come back tomorrow for an interview with him…."

I started to panic. "Oh, I'm sorry. I'm on vacation—with my friend, in the waiting room—and we have plans for tomorrow."

She excused herself again.

"The manager could see you in twenty minutes, if you could wait."

"Oh, I'm sure we can't. It will be very inconvenient. But I *will* ask my friend and see what her schedule is."

With the interviewer one step behind me, I greeted Marcella, reading a magazine in a small waiting room. I kept my voice calm but feverishly contorted my face as if I were telling Marcella to lead the way out the door. "They'd like to know if we can wait twenty minutes for a second interview, but we don't have time, do we?"

Marcella smiled and threw her hands up in the air. "No problem. We can wait."

I sat down next to Marcella, no longer sure I counted her among my friends. "Why are you so dead-set against the idea?" she asked. "You say you want to improve your situation, so why not improve it in Portland?"

"I've grown to like the desert," I answered, digging myself into the sand.

Did I really believe this? What had happened to the adventuresome Eileen who had set out from North Carolina on a Greyhound bus and enjoyed the ride? Had life knocked that young woman unconscious? I set aside the niggling questions.

An hour later, I breathed a sigh of relief to be walking down a sidewalk away from that federal building, never to return—or so I thought.

Back home in Tucson, an apologetic VA manager arranged a private conversation and broke the news: I'd been the top candidate for the "dream" social work services job—until a woman applied who held that very same position at another VA hospital. "I'm sorry, but…"

I was tired of hearing the words.

I held my composure until he walked out of the room, then I shut the door and sobbed out my disappointment and anger. Anger at God. Through all my trials I'd remained confident that He existed, but right then I had no assurance that He knew I existed. In case He knew, I inwardly railed: *Why don't You let me better myself? What do You want of me? I'm sick of trying. Show me what You want!*

Show me what You want! That very afternoon Portland called. The OPM job was mine. I'd have one week's paid leave to make my cross-country move. Could I start immediately?

Panicked but too polite to give an outright no, I strung one excuse after another. I wasn't listening. I was too afraid.

"Oh, I can't possibly resign here and pack and move and be up there in one week."

"I'll see what I can do," he said, and called back with authorization to give me two weeks of paid leave. "So," he said, "you could start December 26?"

"Oh, I can't possibly leave right at Christmas and not be here with my family."

"Okay… could you start January 2?"

"I couldn't possibly be traveling on the highway over New Year's, not with all the holiday drinking."

Understandably, this man sounded annoyed, so annoyed I was sure he'd withdraw his offer.

He called back two days later. "We've put our heads together, and we think we can work with you. Can you start on January 14?"

I almost said "No, that's my son's birthday." But I simply couldn't. Not when I'd asked God for direction. Not when my son and friends were telling me to go—go north. "Try it for one year," my son said. "If you don't like it, then come back. You'd be able to get back into the VA. What have you got to lose?"

"Yes, I'll be there on January 14," I told Portland. It had taken me a long time, but finally I let myself hear God's answer. I said yes to the persistent voice.

On Tuesday, January 8, 1980, I packed possessions into every available inch of the beige station wagon. On Tuesday morning I sent my son off to work, said good-bye to the Tucson Mountains, and headed on a journey that would take me northwest on Interstate 10, west on Interstate 8, then Interstate 5, up through California's wide valleys, with a side trip through narrow mountain passes to visit friends who provided me with a night's lodging.

A winter rain set in along the way, a hard rain that made driving difficult and made me worry all over again about whether I was doing the right thing. I'd grip the wheel and ask God for yet another sign that I should continue filling the insatiable gas tank. Then I'd try to focus my mind back on the calming psalm: "Be still and know." I could say it to the rhythm of the windshield wipers.

On Wednesday, I kept driving. But so did the rain. With the wipers flicking fast, I shifted into low as I headed through a mountain pass called the Grapevine, north of Los Angeles on I-5. *Should I just turn around and go back? God, tell me what to do!* Today the wipers clicked a conflicting message: Yes-no. Yes-no. Yes-no.

Coming down off the Grapevine, I turned on the radio, hoping to hear a song or a weather report to soothe my nerves. I wasn't expecting a sign from God, but that's what I got. Not fifteen minutes later an announcer reported that a mudslide had closed the northbound lanes of the Grapevine—the very pass I'd just come through. I gasped. *Why now? Why not thirty minutes ago—when it could have blocked my path? It's a sign. Okay, Lord, I'll keep driving.*

The real test of my determination came Friday morning. I headed into the Siskiyou Mountain range. It was still raining, but now there was talk of snow. Being a Southerner, I knew winter-driving perils by reputation only. As I pulled out of Redding early Friday morning, the motel manager said, "No matter what, easy does it."

I was too revved up to eat breakfast. *Just got to get on the road. Just got to get on the other side of that mountain.* An hour into my trip, as I hugged the inside of an upgrade mountain curve, the rain turned white. So did my knuckles.

Too soon the side of the road, even the side of the mountain, was strewn with stranded cars. Occasionally, a tow truck with chains tugged at a car that had slid over the bank; distressed travelers huddled and hoped as the front grille of their car was winched onto the road.

Easy does it. Easy does it. *Lord, I'll keep my hands on the wheel. Are You there on the remote control?*

Suddenly, right ahead of me, a semitrailer eased onto the highway from an entrance ramp. And for an hour those huge tire treads marked the trail for me. Every once in a while my back wheels would lose traction and spin. Easy does it, they'd grab again, and get me over the next ridge—until, midmorning, I knew I would be among the marooned if I didn't find gas, soon.

The gauge slipped closer and closer to empty, as I followed my trucker-guide past one exit then another, some blocked by vehicles, some with ramps so steep I didn't dare....

And then I saw one more of those blue signs: "Gas and Food." Yes! The road was clear and both the off and on ramps amazingly flat. *Thank You, Lord.*

In terms of this exit, "gas and food" said it all. The road led to a filling station and a small restaurant next door. There, at the end of the tiny box canyon, the wilderness began. The road ended.

Standing in snow that buried my feet, I pumped my own gas. I turned away from the wind and looked toward the white sky. For a fleeting moment, I forgot my fears and let the cold flakes melt against my cheeks. As I relaxed, my thoughts turned to food and the breakfast I hadn't eaten. I was hungry. *I'll take a break and eat. Maybe pancakes and link sausages.*

Inside, out of the gale, I handed cash to the young attendant. "I guess I'll get some breakfast over here." I nodded toward the restaurant.

"Do you mind if I give you some advice?" she asked, staring straight into my eyes. She didn't wait for my answer. "This storm is not over. You still have lots of mountain country. The time you waste here eating could make the difference. I suggest you keep on going."

I stared back at her. Her clear blue eyes shone with a concern for me that I found as sincere as it was urgent. "Yes," I said, "that's what I'll do. Thank you. I'll eat later."

The rest of the morning I drove with a little more confidence, and about noon I descended below the snow line, into Ashland, Oregon. I stopped to eat there.

Later in the afternoon, I stopped again for gas. This time I could pick my brand of gas, and stopped at a Mobil station, on the right, within sight of the highway. The road cut through a small hamlet and headed east into farm country and rolling hills. The proprietor was a chatty, tall man, older than I, who took an interest in my old but well-kept car, its Arizona plates, and its weighty load. As he pumped the gas for me, we chatted cheerfully.

He wore glasses, and through them I could see clear blue eyes that were more twinkly than shiny. "You're headed for Portland," he said. I couldn't tell whether it was a statement or a question.

"Yes," I said. Still holding the nozzle, he turned his head toward me. "Do you mind if I give you some advice? You don't know this country," he continued. "By four o'clock it's going to be pitch dark and when they're wet the roads can be treacherous. Get off the highway by three o'clock, wherever you are."

"I'll keep that in mind," I replied. "Thank you."

Do you mind if I give you some advice? Those were the same words the young woman in the box canyon had used. I'd followed her advice. She'd been right to urge me on.

My original plan had been to get to Portland that night. But at three o'clock I thought about the gas station attendant's words, "Get off the highway." I was drawing close to the city of Eugene. I did have the phone number of a Tucson friend's daughter. "When you drive through Eugene, stop and give her a call," the mother had said.

And from a pay phone off the interstate, I dialed the number. *Thank God it's stopped raining*, I thought, letting my mind wander as the phone rang and rang and rang. Just returning the receiver to the hook, I heard a breathless "hello" and the young woman's explanation: on her way out but hearing the phone, she'd run back in to answer.

"Where are you?" she asked, eager to change her plans, come meet me, and lead me across town to her home. And there, joining her for a dinner party, I was warmly welcomed, as if all the open arms of Oregon were bidding me to enter.

I spent the night there and on Saturday morning, at last, my destination was in sight. I headed north for the last three-hour leg of my trip. Finally, the roads were dry, but north of Eugene the landscape grew inexplicably desolate:

snow-banked berms, snapped telephone polls and evergreens, closed roads, and detoured traffic.

At the end of my journey, I sat quietly for a few minutes in Marcella's driveway. Shallow, wide steps invited me into the huge, oak double doorway of the natural-wood cedar home. I surveyed my new temporary home, its yard dotted with evergreens, everything from deep-green giants down to small Christmas trees. *Yes, I will make a home here,* I thought. *I no longer need the desert. It's time to find beauty in the forest.*

I finally awoke from my reverie and climbed the steps. When Marcella opened her door, she wasn't her usual laid-back self. She greeted me with open but tense arms. "We've been worried sick about you." Then she told me how Oregon had just been hit by the worst ice storm of the century. "A train is still marooned in the Columbia River gorge. They're dropping supplies by helicopter. We didn't know where you were. We've been praying constantly."

I walked into Marcella's house having no doubt but that God had given me the confirmation I needed to continue my trip with confidence. At the center of my being I could be still—knowing that God was a God Who could make his purposes clear.

I came to Oregon fifteen years ago, and I've never seriously regretted the move. My OPM boss was the world's best. When he retired and Reagan Administration cutbacks threatened my job, I easily transferred to another federal agency, a substantial upgrade that involved interacting with people, investigating leads, and writing reports, things I love to do.

Of course, I've returned to Arizona to visit my children and grandchildren. (I've brought north a few more of my prized possessions.) And I've driven I-5 through the Siskiyou Mountains a number of times. Last winter I went down and back through northern California and looked once more, carefully, for a "Gas and Food" sign and a grade-level exit to a box-canyon, dead-end road. I haven't been able to find it yet. What's more, there is no highway-side hamlet that in any way resembles the one with the Mobil station run by the older man with dancing eyes.

Were those advice-giving angels? That's what I now choose to believe. They were like the heavenly messenger described in Exodus 23, sent by God to the wandering children of Israel "to guard you along the way and to bring you to the place I have prepared." But that Scripture continues with a command: "Pay attention to him and listen to what he says."

Sometimes I've been stubborn, hard to convince, but I've learned how to listen with confidence. That's what I want my granddaughter Vanessa to know about and to take to heart.

Facing the first days of my latest adventure, retirement at age sixty-nine, I contemplate two underlying messages I heard from my Oregon-highway angels. Each, I see, was tailored to my situation in a particular time and place: A blue-eyed woman told me to keep moving; don't dawdle. A bespeckled man told me that I shouldn't push it; stop.

As I listened to God, and my doctor, my first retirement message was a clear "slow down." An unexpectedly long recovery from optic surgery had forced me to stay close to home for more than a month. Those quiet days were hard for me; I still have itchy feet. I want to get out and travel—see Mount Rushmore, set foot in Minnesota, tour Canada coast to coast.

Yet every morning, while still in bed, I remind myself to be still and to listen. I pray, "Lord, I'm ready to go. I'm ready for the happy surprises You have in store for me today."

With God, you never know what the next adventure will be.

Roberta Messner

AT THE AGE OF FIFTEEN, Roberta Messner experienced a number of seizures and blackouts that were found to be caused by a disease called neurofibromatosis, popularly known as the "Elephant Man's Disease." Painful, disfiguring, nerve- and vision-impairing tumors developed in Roberta's head. In the days and years that followed, there would be surgical operations to endure, many of them. Today she is a woman in her early forties. She lives in Sweet Run, West Virginia, with her husband Mark and their dog Cleo. The disease is still with her—there is no cure—and though she is in the hospital almost every day, it is not because of neurofibromatosis.

Roberta is a registered nurse with a Ph.D.; she puts her knowledge to use by specializing in nursing quality management. In her work in nearby Hunting- ton, she has found that her own medical trials have given her an invaluable personal perspective on how to improve patient satisfaction with health care. She has written a book on the subject, hardly her first venture into publishing, for Roberta is a veteran writer with a nursing textbook and a long list of articles on her résumé. She has written on all kinds of subjects, everything from medical matters to inspirational themes. Also, she is a field editor for home decorating magazines. As a photo stylist, she scouts out houses and interiors and other subjects that would make good picture opportunities.

"I live on the edge of expectancy," Roberta has said about herself. She expects good things to happen. You can sense the sunniness in her through her writing, including the happy-hearted story about her father here. Yet there are always moments when the darkness closes in. In late 1993 and early 1994, she underwent three operations to remove more tumors growing inside her head. One growth behind her eye was so large that her sight was seriously endangered.

"Shortly before the surgery for that, I panicked," she admits. "I called an 800 prayer line and asked for a big load of prayers—that there would be no nerve damage, that I would not lose an inordinate amount of blood, that my vision would be safe, that—" The man on the other end of the line interrupted her.

"God wants to supply *all* your needs," he said, trying to be helpful and soothing, "but, Roberta, what *one* thing would you ask Him for?"

Roberta hesitated, then something came to mind. It seemed so unimportant that she felt a little foolish asking God for it. She remembered how cold and frightening the operating rooms had always been for her when she first entered them. If there were just some way to avoid facing that first chill….

On the morning of the operation an orderly helped her onto the gurney, then wheeled her toward the operating room. "When we pass through the double doors," he told her, "the temperature is going to drop significantly. But don't you worry, someone will be waiting on the other side with a soft, heated blanket."

And that's exactly the way it was.

Roberta believes in the heavenly angels God sends on occasion to answer prayers, and she believes in His human angels, like the orderly and the nurse who was waiting with the soft, warm blanket. In the medical profession she feels privileged to serve in, Roberta is well aware of being surrounded by angels. They are the skilled caregivers who mind and mend and work for improved quality of life.

All the while Roberta knows that there is a dark shadow hanging over her life, for it never leaves. "But I also have a guardian angel up there," she says. "I have never seen my angel, but I can tell you this: Its brightness puts my shadow to shame."

Manna in the Wilderness

by Roberta Messner

[The children of Israel] spoke against God, saying,
"Can God spread a table in the wilderness?
He smote the rock so that water gushed out
and streams overflowed.
Can he also give bread,
or provide meat for this people?"...
[God] commanded the skies above,
and opened the doors of heaven;
and he rained down upon them manna to eat,
and gave them the grain of heaven.
Man ate of the bread of the angels;
he sent them food in abundance....
And they ate and were well filled,
for he gave them what they craved.

—Psalm 78:19-20, 23-25, 29 (RSV)

IKE HUNDREDS OF THOUSANDS of other nostalgia seekers, my dad's favorite Labor Day weekend event was the huge flea market in Hillsville, Virginia. For fifteen years he'd packed up his treasures and rehearsed his music and tales and headed south, from Huntington, West Virginia, down the Blue Ridge Mountains.

His destination? A twelve-acre weed field overrun with trucks and vans and jalopies jammed so close they were landlocked for four days. From tailgates and tables, over six hundred vendors from all over the country traded their collectibles and told their stories. Dad's specialty? Violins. Come evening, a strip of grass at one end of the midway became a bandstand, where my dad and his buddies fiddled away the night.

But in the summer of 1989, my dad was diagnosed with cancer. By the first of September he was in the middle of heavy-duty radiation therapy. The seven-mile ride to the local hospital and back home each morning wiped him out for the entire day.

Living just a few miles from my folks, I stopped in nearly every evening after I got off work at the hospital where I was a registered nurse. The week before Labor Day weekend, I pulled Mom aside on the porch. While Dad dozed in his living room recliner, I whispered, "I don't see how he can possibly go to Hillsville this year," I said. "Especially with the scorching weather they're predicting. Look how weak and short-winded he is. And that's here in the house, where he sits in his recliner all day. If he gets sick in Virginia, it's going to be one big mess. Once you've parked on that midway, there's no getting out. You're landlocked. What would he do?"

"Honey, I wish he'd reconsider, too. But you know your dad. Once he's got his mind made up, there's no changing it," Mom said. "He's looked forward to this trip all year long."

Still, Mom and I and my younger sister Rebekkah reasoned and cajoled and begged Dad to cancel his trip.

No. He was going. And he convinced his doctor to postpone a Friday radiation treatment—on one condition, that someone go with him.

Afraid that he'd pack his precious violins into his van, hop in, and head south alone despite the doctor's orders, Rebekkah and I quickly juggled our work schedules and got the weekend off. With health problems of her own, Mom wasn't up to making the trip. We reserved a motel room near Hillsville, close enough to keep an eye on Dad without pestering him. I packed a satchel full of his prescriptions and other potions that might relieve distress. There was the pink stuff, the chalky stuff, fizz-fizz tablets.... And Mom packed a cooler full of Dad's favorite sandwiches, salads, and snack foods.

Propelled by sheer willpower, Dad got up before dawn on Friday and packed his van for the three-hour trip south to Hillsville.

"Now you be sure and eat to keep your strength up," Mom instructed, kissing Dad good-bye. "And sip on one of those cold Seven-Ups when you're out in the sun." As Mom hugged Rebekkah and me, she added, "You all just go and have a good time—and don't worry. I'm trusting God to take care of things while your dad's so far from home. It will all work out. You'll see."

Then she handed us two big, brown, empty shopping bags. "Can't wait to see what you come home with," she added, the porch light burning in the background. That was Mom—always expecting an empty bag to be filled to overflowing with blessings.

Rebekkah and I followed in my Oldsmobile, discussing contingency plans, what we were going to do with Dad if—or when—the trip got the best of him. We also whiled away the hours imagining what finds we'd buy. Years before I'd been to the Hillsville market with my husband Mark, looking for vintage household decorations and parts for his old truck. Now I had a more serious interest in antiques: In addition to my nursing career, I was a part-time photo stylist for several country-style decorating publications. I hoped to uncover some great photo props. And Rebekkah, she was always trying to add milk bottles and Shirley Temple memorabilia to her collections.

While Dad found his spot in the market morass—turf he'd earned by squatter's rights—we parked along the side of the road and walked twenty minutes to the entrance gate.

Once inside the gate, we quickly tracked down Dad and helped him drag his folding table, green canvas umbrella, and violin cases from the van. "You girls go ahead and mill around and let me do this," Dad insisted, beads of perspiration forming on his forehead. "I'm not an invalid yet."

We sat on a patch of grass and talked to the vendor next to Dad about the costume rings he was selling. "I'll keep a close eye on your father," he promised when Dad wasn't listening. "He's really gone downhill since last year."

About that time a squirmy kid wearing coveralls and a red bandanna moseyed up to the table with his mother to check out Dad's fiddles. "You play the violin, young man?" Dad asked.

The boy, maybe eight, nodded sheepishly.

"I was about your age when I tried my hand at it, son. Learned on a two-dollar model from Sears and Roebuck. Back on the farm we didn't have much to entertain us except music. Pick one of these out and play me a tune." Dad tapped his feet as the kid squeaked "Little Brown Jug." "Why, you'll be fiddling 'Soldier's Joy' before you know it," Dad said through a strained smile, steadying himself on the edge of the teetering metal table.

To hunt up the rest rooms Rebekkah and I left Dad, decked out in a big straw farmer's hat and sagging in his folding chair. We swung back by his table to give him some advice on the contents of the medicine satchel. "If you get the least bit nauseated in this heat," I cautioned, "be sure and take a dose of that Maalox."

"Maybe you better take a couple of Tylenols now, just in case," Rebekkah piped up. "Here's a bit of Mom's good ol' potato salad to chase them down with."

Dad obliged. "Okay, mother hens, did you crack your car windows? Be sure and put some sunblock on your face and arms, and get yourselves something cold to drink every little bit. Where's your hats? There's no shade in this place...."

We laughed and left to comb the aisles, searching for any old, red-handled kitchen utensils or Shirley Temple collectibles. We frequently checked in on Dad, then we'd wander off, through the wilderness of discards, until worry got the best of us again. Then we'd swing back around. Each time he looked fine, though he wasn't shooting the breeze with potential customers.

After we'd eaten a corn dog and fries lunch, Rebekkah fixed Dad a sandwich, which he turned down. And the guy parked next to Dad pulled me aside.

"I think you should know that your dad hasn't eaten a bite all day," he said in a confidential whisper. "He sits with his head in his hands until he spots you two coming. Then he tries to pretend like nothing's wrong."

I went back to chat with Dad and asked him about a tin pail at his feet. "In case I get sick to my stomach," he explained.

The nurse in me couldn't pretend any longer. "Dad, if you don't eat a little something, you're going to get even weaker.... Isn't there *something* you'd try to eat?"

"There is one thing I keep thinking about," he answered. "An old-time country dinner—the salt-side ham we used to eat on the farm. There's nothing like that around here, I'm sure."

"I haven't seen any, but you never know," I said. "We'll go ask and see what we can find."

"Who can figure that?" I said as Rebekkah and I headed to the nearest concession stand. "As sick as he is, and he wants some home-cured Virginia ham."

We found hot dogs, hush puppies, and funnel cakes, but nothing resembling Dad's request.

Returning to give him a report, we passed a vendor displaying white wicker furniture. For sale at the next booth was a big-ticket dining room suite with chairs decorated with carved lions' heads. The next man was peddling turquoise and red feedsacks that said Dixieland. I snatched one up as a birthday gift for my friend Dixie.

And next to him a long table covered with rainbow-hued glassware strangely beckoned us under a green and white striped canopy. As we admired the hodgepodge of dishes and knickknacks, a woman with white, wispy hair wearing a blue calico apron spoke to us. "You girls hang around a minute," she instructed before disappearing inside a camper.

Seconds later, she opened the door and walked down the steps carrying a paper plate heaped with food and a tall Styrofoam cup of iced tea. "Virginia-baked ham for your dad," she explained, handing me the plate.

Rebekkah and I stared at each other. Rebekkah stifled a giggle behind her hand. "I can't believe it," I said under my breath, spying Dad's favorite fluffy lemon meringue pie for dessert.

The grandmotherly woman explained, "I added a pinch of pepper to the potatoes and black-eyed peas. Sure hope he gets to feeling better." For a brief moment the shade under the striped canopy was as cozy as a farmhouse kitchen, a pull-up-your-chair kind of place.

Rebekkah interrupted my reverie. "Oh, boy, iced tea! Could I get one with Sweet'n Low and no lemon?" she asked.

The woman shook her head. "No, honey. I made this tea just for your dad," she said softly.

"Here, let me pay you."

The woman shook her head and planted her hands in her apron pockets.

"This is the kindest thing that's ever happened to me at a flea market," I said. "You know, I work for a few magazines. I should write a story about this. People need to know about folks like you."

An angelic smile crossed the lady's face. "You do that," she said. "You just do that."

Like excited schoolgirls, we rushed across the aisles to Dad's table to present him with our find. "*Psst.* Wait till we get home, and I tell Mom she's got a little competition here," Rebekkah kidded, giddy with delight.

"Dad, your friend up the way sent you this," I explained. "A small lady about your age. White hair. She has eyes that look right inside your heart. I guess we didn't get her name."

He perked up and accepted the gifts. "Don't know anybody by that description," he said as he sipped his tea. "Say, since when did you learn to sweeten my tea just the way I like it?"

"The woman did it, not me."

"Well, run back and find out who she is. And thank her for all this." He sank his teeth into a slice of warm ham.

Dutiful daughters, Rebekkah and I retraced our steps, crossing through several aisles to find the canopy. There, next to the Dixieland feedsack dealer, we saw not the green and white canopy but an unfamiliar brown pickup truck. A man, dressed in a T-shirt and cut-off jeans, was selling old lamps. We talked to the feedsack dealer. How could the canopy and camper have fled the scene so quickly? And where was the elderly lady?

"Been here all day," he said. "Haven't seen anyone like that. And that truck pulled in here same time I did this morning. You girls sure you know what you're talking about?"

Rebekkah hummed the theme from *The Twilight Zone* as we noodled along back to Dad.

As we got close to his van, we both noticed that he wasn't there. *Now what?* I thought, expecting the worst.

But his neighbor next door grinned as he gave his report. "Your dad just sailed his empty paper plate into that trash can and took off to do some Christmas shopping. Asked me to watch his table for him. Says he's planning on playing his fiddle after the sun goes down."

We started laughing. "I'd like to know what was in that food," Rebekkah said. "That lady was nowhere to be found when we went back to thank her. Everyone we asked about her looked at us as if we had completely lost touch with reality."

Dad's neighbor stared into the distance as if he was contemplating the universe. "Manna from heaven, that's what I think. It's right in the Bible, you know. The hungry Israelites were wandering in the wilderness, wishing they were back home in Egypt. Then food dropped right from the sky."

We stayed at Dad's table until he came back—which wasn't for about an hour. We hovered over him. "Dad, how you doing? Here, have a seat. Here, take a drink."

But he was smiling and joking and hardly winded—like his old self. But not exactly. The old Dad would never have held out his hand and placed in my palm a gift he'd bought himself, a women's gold, Victorian, pocket-style watch to wear on a gold chain.

"What's gotten into him?" Rebekkah whispered as Dad tidied up his table, whistling an old mountain tune.

He turned to Rebekkah. "And I tried to find you a Shirley Temple doll. This isn't the year, honey. Nobody had a thing."

"Now, you girls can go home now. No need to baby-sit any longer. I'm doing good enough to be here on my own."

We were not convinced, so the next day we drove two hours south to check out another flea market. When we returned, Dad convinced us to drive on home. And he took care of himself the rest of the weekend.

When Dad pulled into the driveway Monday evening, he was whistling as he unloaded the van, Mom said. And the satchel hadn't been touched the rest of the weekend, despite our well-meaning potions and contingency plans. Just as Mom predicted, God had taken care of everything.

A ministering spirit. As time passed, Rebekkah and I had no other explanation for the calico woman we couldn't track down. Hadn't God fed Elijah by sending ravens? And, yes, for forty years God provided the Israelites with manna that appeared every morning like dew on the grass. Surely He was capable of sending an elderly woman with a plateful of Virginia ham, as unlikely as a supernatural, ministering presence seemed in that swampland turned flea market.

I treasured the watch my dad bought me in Hillsville, but wanting another remembrance of that day, a few years later I purchased an old guardian-angel lithograph I came across in an antique shop in Columbus, Ohio. A young barefoot boy and girl are huddled on a wooden footbridge, traveling toward a cottage in the distance. It's dusk and there's a storm brewing, and they don't see that part of the decking is missing on the bridge. The scene depicts danger: They could fall through the bridge or get struck by lightning at any minute. And yet…if they only knew…an angel is directing their every step home, to safety.

I hung that painting above the Victorian-style mantel in my guest bedroom, hoping it would comfort and strengthen visitors who found shelter under my roof. If they were far from their home, I wanted the lesson to be clear: *You might not see him, but God's angel is nearby, ready to provide for your needs.*

But, actually, I was the one who needed a reminder of the lesson.

Last fall I had to travel to a medical center in a distant city for surgery to remove a large tumor behind my eye. Like those children in my angel picture, there were dangers at every turn. As a nurse, I knew some of them—uncontrollable bleeding, nerve damage and disfiguration, blindness. Other worries— the what ifs—gnawed away at my assurance that God would take care of me. My suitcase was strewn on the guest bed, and Rebekkah helped me fill it with gowns, a robe, slippers. I'd traveled to the city for previous surgeries—and always before Mom, Dad, and Rebekkah had accompanied me. This time, Mark and I would be making the trip alone.

Or would we? Though Rebekkah and I avoided each other's eyes, we were able to focus our attention on the angel picture above the mantel. "Remember our angel," Rebekkah reminded. "Look how things worked out for Dad. The doctors say he's still in remission."

I telephoned home before surgery. "We're praying for you every minute," Dad assured me. And when I entered the unknown world of the operating room, I knew: There are frightening and unfamiliar places we must all travel, humanly speaking, alone. My family's strong faith had helped prepare me for this moment. And besides, in the wilderness of my heart, there was the comforting memory of an angel.

No sickness can come near to blast my health;
My life depends not upon any meat;
My bread comes not from any human tilth;
No wings will grow upon my changeless wealth;
Wrong cannot touch it, violence or deceit;
Thou art my life, my health, my bank, my barn—
And from all other gods thou plain dost warn.
—George MacDonald

Shirley LeMay

IF YOU EVER GET A CHANCE TO TALK to Shirley LeMay, you're in for a good time. She's just plain fun. And when she gets together with her sister, Lena McDonald, it's double the fun.

They're different, of course, as Shirley will explain, but there are many similarities, too. They're both widows; they both love to talk about the good Lord and the old times, good and bad; both are transplanted Texans living in Virginia (Shirley in Arlington, Lena seventy-five miles away in Culpeper). They talk on the telephone at least once a day; Shirley says her fingers know how to dial Lena's number "by heart."

Their father was a Methodist evangelist who would get his family of five children up early and sit them around a table where from 5:00 to 7:00 A.M. they would read and discuss the Bible. ("We'd go straight through from Genesis to Revelation, and when that was done, we'd start all over again.") You can see why it is that the Bible is still an integral part of the *Reverend* Lena McDonald's life. For years she has been a minister in the Full Gospel Fellowship, working tirelessly in hospitals, jails, and Bible study groups. She still has her fifteen-minute Bible program coming out of Chattanooga's WLMR radio station on Saturday mornings. On Sundays, Shirley likes to drive up and go to Lena's Assembly of God Church there in Culpeper.

Shirley is a great-grandmother six times over. Her husband, George Willard LeMay, died in 1990, just a few months short of their fiftieth wedding anniversary. For a long time Shirley made herself useful—and some extra money—by being a school crossing guard. And for seventeen years she was a first-aid instructor "until my knees caught on to my age, then I had to stop." Recently, she heard there was a little money to be made by picking up new cars at Baltimore Harbor and delivering them to area dealerships. Since she loved to drive and had a spotless record, she applied for the job. A Volvo dealer nearby agreed to take her on, but when they told her there might be some long-distance driving involved, she backed out. "I get sleepy if the drive is too long. Anyway, I have a bad sense of direction. I can get lost in a corner drugstore with only one exit."

Lately, Shirley has been thinking that she might pick up that needed extra cash at flea markets. She owns about five thousand books in her house that ought to be worth something. "They're all clean books," she points out, "old-type westerns like Zane Grey. Jack London's *Call of the Wild*. Lots of light romances, which were wonderful reading before they started getting dirty."

Shirley has this to say about the story she has written: "I guess I really have *seen* my angel at last. I can't prove it, of course, but in my mind there isn't any doubt. It's another reason for being joyful about our wonderful Savior's provisions. I just bubble over with joy when I talk about my angels. They are old friends to me."

Not that there is ever a final word between the two sisters, but Lena did have this to say to Shirley: "If that's your guardian angel, you sure have a good-looking one."

The Tale of Two Sisters

by Shirley LeMay

Father, we thank You for Your graciousness,
for Your angels that protect us on Earth's vast
spaciousness;
for their blocking the sight of an enemy strong,
for their standing around us, when all else goes wrong.
They see what's coming from around the bend,
to keep Your children from an untimely end.
Again, we thank You and say amen.

—Shirley LeMay

 ALWAYS LOOK FORWARD TO A DAY'S OUTING with my older sister, Lena McDonald. We're both talkers, and we have a grand old time. We reminisce about the Depression childhood we shared in the wilds of western Texas. We talk about our husbands, now deceased, and the journeys that brought us both to our homes in northern Virginia. We talk about our similar health problems. We discuss our children and how they're raising theirs. And every conversation includes a reverent reference to our good God.

This might sound as if we have a lot in common. Well, we do, but we don't. If you saw us walking down the street, you might notice a resemblance in our aging features. But that's about all. My sister dresses like a store mannequin. She's a minister who looks ever-ready to step up to a pulpit and preach. Perfect composure. Hair always coifed. Pumps always shined, with a handbag to match.

Me, I'm different. I prefer comfort to fashion. And I don't go in for much fussing. When I'm going out, I run a comb through my hair. My all-purpose shoes protect my feet and support my arches. I can't remember when I last plugged in a flatiron. Of course, there are some things I'm very particular about. I like my name pronounced right. It's *Le*May, not LaMay. Someone says it wrong, and I'll correct him or her real quick. And I like to travel in my own car. That way I have a little sense of control. When Lena and I spend a day together, we take my Dodge minivan, and I drive.

One cool Saturday morning in April 1994, Lena drove an hour east from her home in Culpeper, Virginia, to my house, about a mile from the Pentagon. About ten I saw her pull into my paved driveway. *We shouldn't stand around and chat*, I thought. *We need to get on the road.* We had a long drive ahead of us, one hundred miles each way to the veterans' hospital in northern Maryland. A friend of Lena's was dying of cancer, and I'd offered to take her to visit. My car, of course. I threw on my lightweight jacket and picked up my purse. I travel light, and I was ready to go.

Lena, on the other hand, who knows what she's got in those tote bags that she always transfers from her car to mine? You'd think she was going camping for six weeks. Like a scout, she likes to be prepared. "You never know, I might need something," she says.

As I waited, she fiddled with the key and the lock of the trunk. When she couldn't get it open, she turned to the wonders of modern convenience. Turning the ignition key to engage the electrical system, she pushed a button and popped the trunk open. Mission accomplished, she slammed the car door and moved her precious possessions to the backseat of my van.

That day our conversation seemed stuck in one groove: angels. The topic came up as a result of my having just missed yet another mammoth pothole on Interstate 95. (We Texans call them "chugholes.") When I swerved but managed to stay in my lane, I uttered an automatic, "Thank You, Lord," to which Lena added a concurring, "Thank You." She always does that. But I added something of my own. "The angels are looking after us today," I said. And that started us talking about them. We stopped for comfort and coffee at a restaurant along I-95. Even there we kept up the conversation; we still had angels on our mind.

As long as I can remember, I've known I had guardian angels. My dad died when I was eleven. He didn't leave us much in the way of earthly possessions, but he left a godly heritage. He would tell me that I had an angel. And I believed him. Lena did, too, but since I'm the one telling our story....

I'd never knowingly seen an angel. But time and again when I've been in danger, I've felt an unexplainable protection. Like the day I was home alone and climbed the tall tree in my backyard. I wanted to pick every last one of those cherries to freeze for cobblers and pies. (Lena would *never* climb a cherry tree, even as a child.) When I'd taken my balancing act as high as the second story windows, I looked down to pull up my empty bucket, which was tied to the kite string attached to my belt. The string caught on a tiny twig, and then I let go of the branch above. Bad move. At that very moment the branch under my foot snapped. What held me up in that tree? A piece of kite string bore my entire weight, and not for just a second. The more I tried to regain my balance, the more taut it became. At last! I grabbed hold of a secure branch.

At the time I thanked God and didn't think in terms of an angel's direct intervention. But years later I actually *felt* the messenger.

It was the winter of 1990, just months after my husband had died. Our house has always been air-conditioned—by God's breath. Summer or winter, the wind comes right through the walls. This particular week, I set the alarm every two hours all night so I could check the wood fire. At 4:00 A.M. I shivered out of bed and went to the long, narrow back porch to get a load of wood. If I was careful, I could carry four slabs at a time.

This time I wasn't careful enough. With my arms full, I caught my toe in the threadbare throw rug. My feet stopped, but my torso fell full length toward the closed door between the porch and kitchen. I heard the wood click against the door's glass. I put one hand out to catch myself and touched something soft and warm. I felt unseen hands push back on my shoulders, and instantly I was standing upright, my back against a wall that had been not directly behind me but to my left.

As cold as it was, the next morning I checked out that porch, looking for something soft and warm. The softest thing I could find was the rug I'd tripped on. And warm was out of the question.

Though I'd *felt* an angel, I can't say that I'd ever seen an angel until...

Having visited Lena's friend in Maryland, we drove back into my driveway just before dusk. Lena unloaded her bags from my van, pulled out a set of keys from her purse and opened the car door. A brief beep warned her of trouble. She'd left a second set of keys in the ignition with the electrical system engaged, and the heater fan on. Lena grimaced and turned the key. She heard that awful click, click, click. She wasn't going anywhere in her Oldsmobile. The battery was dead.

"Not to worry," said her son Billy on the telephone, long distance. "There's a set of jumper cables in the trunk. I put them there myself. Never been used. Just hook them up to Aunt Shirley's van and you're home free."

I was standing beside Lena, listening to one end of this conversation. I cut in real fast. "There's no way we can do it ourselves." Lena handed me the phone. "Billy, one day years back a mechanic tried to jump-start our car. He got things wrong and the car engine went up in a puff of smoke. You've got to know what you're doing. And we ladies don't."

Lena got back on the line. "Mom, tell Aunt Shirley to simmer down. It's real simple. The cables are color-coded to the posts on the battery, and anybody can do it."

I was still skeptical, but what were we to do? I wielded my "sheriff's special" flashlight that takes six D batteries. Lena in her high heels and I in my black casuals dug out the cables from the back corner of the trunk.

Yes, they were color-coded.

Yes, there were two sets of alligator clips. But still I hesitated. I'm the kind of person who doesn't mind asking for help when I need it, so I turned around and canvassed the street looking for aid. There's a restaurant next door and a street of shops across the street. Usually there's quite a bit of pedestrian traffic. Not tonight. No one, respectable looking or not, in sight. We would have to do the thing ourselves.

I can turn my van around on a dime, and I maneuvered it in place, my front left bumper to her right bumper with walking room between us. I unlatched and lifted the hood, picked up one end of the cables and tried to squeeze open the alligator clips. They were brand-new. I didn't have the strength in my hand to get them open. Now I was really at a loss. That's when from behind me, toward the street but right in the yard, I heard a man's voice. "You ladies look like you're having some difficulty. Can I be of help?"

I turned around. "Yes, please," I said.

About six feet from me stood a young man I'd never seen before. Neither tall nor short, in his twenties. The most beautiful blue eyes you've ever seen. *A college kid*, I thought. *Where'd he come from?* He was dressed in his Saturday clothes: jeans, a plaid sports shirt open at the collar. A variegated knit hat covered all his hair, but I could see blond eyebrows. He carried himself like a real gentleman.

I handed him my end of the cables and Lena started asking questions. "What are you doing here?" she asked. "Where did you come from?"

I don't think he answered her, but he had such a winning smile that Lena reluctantly handed him her end of the cables.

With no effort, the stranger opened the alligator clips. With my car still running, he rigged up the cables, first to Lena's dead car, then to my live wire. "We don't usually do it this way," he said, "but we can handle it." I've since heard that one normally clamps the cable to the batteries with both cars turned off.

"Start your motor now," he told Lena, command in his voice.

The engine turned over but then died.

He just smiled and said, "Try again."

I can tell you Lena isn't used to taking orders. But she complied, and the spark took. The motor purred.

"Thank the Lord that motor started," I said.

"I'm glad you know Whom to thank," he answered.

Within seconds, he reached for the clips on Lena's car, as if to disengage the connection. At this, Lena started to fuss at him. "My son said we had to leave the cables on for at least five minutes. It needs more juice. Don't be so hasty."

The man kept smiling. Still very much in charge of the situation, he answered, "Oh, it will run now, just fine. You won't have any more trouble with it."

Now I jumped in. "Even when she turns the lights on?" Within minutes it would be dark.

Lena wanted to get another word in. "Yes, what about my lights?"

He just held his stance. "It will be all right," he assured one more time.

Mission accomplished, he wound up the cables like a hose and put them back in Lena's trunk.

Lena still wanted a little more information. "What's your name? Where do you live?"

The first question he ignored. The second he answered with a vague, "I live around here."

"But where? I've never seen you here in the neighborhood."

That smile never left his face. "Around *here*." He rubbed his hands together as if to remove some grease from his palms.

Giving the trunk lid a good slam, Lena volunteered her name. "I don't think we introduced ourselves. I'm Rev. McDonald, and this is my sister, Mrs. LeMay."

He broke into the most beautiful smile you ever saw. His eyes fairly twinkled, and he looked like he was in on the most lovely joke and couldn't reveal it. "Yes, I know," he said. "Glad to meet you, Mrs. LeMay." He emphasized the long *e* in the first syllable, as if he had seen the name in writing and known it wasn't the more common *LaMay*.

He turned to Lena. "You're free to go now." Lena tensed up a little. Was this young stranger dismissing her? I knew Lena meant to come in and talk awhile before heading back. No matter, she did as he said. She got behind the wheel. As she pulled away, she looked back and saw me standing in the drive. She didn't see the young man, she told me later, though she looked in every direction.

As the young man turned to leave me, I again, quite naturally, referred to the Lord: "Thank God you showed up."

"It *was* fortunate, wasn't it?" he answered.

I reached out and shook his firm hand, which was perfectly clean, not a trace of grease. Then he walked out to my quiet street and turned left, toward the market and the main road. I glanced down at my van, its engine still purring. *You better turn it off*, I thought to myself. *Okay, in just a second.*

When I looked up, the blue-eyed man was gone. I do not see how he could have gotten to the corner in the second I looked away, but he was gone. Just gone.

I turned off the engine and walked through the back porch into my kitchen. *Our God is good*, I thought as I opened the refrigerator to see what I could find for supper. The spring air was warm enough I didn't have to set the alarm to get up at 4:00 A.M.

Nearly every morning about six, Lena calls me just to check in and chat. Her Sunday morning call started with our usual ritual: "You got home okay? Did you sleep well?…"

Finally, Lena said, "Oh, wasn't that a fine-looking young man who helped us last night?"

"Did you notice his eyes?" I asked.

"Yes, and that beautiful smile and the gorgeous blond hair. It's so unusual that someone so dressed up like that would stop and offer to get his hands dirty. That dress shirt and tie was beautiful, don't you think?"

"Lena, you've got to be kidding. He didn't have on a dress shirt and tie. He had on jeans and a sports shirt. He had a stocking cap on his head."

"He did NOT. He was dressed up, like he was going to church. His shoes were shined, his slacks were perfectly pressed, and his hair was combed to

250

perfection." The conversation got a little heated, and Lena didn't appreciate my contradicting her. Eventually, I had the presence of mind to say, "Lena, I know what I saw, and you know what you saw. The two stories don't jibe. We both agree about the man's existence, about his blue eyes, his smile. I agree that his eyebrows were blond." But that was all we agreed on. Lena had seen a young man dressed in entirely different clothes from the one I had seen. We argued for a while and then we agreed to disagree. The conversation drew to a close. Lena and I talk frequently, but it *was* a long-distance call.

Did a heavenly messenger of mercy jump-start Lena's car in my own front yard? The more I thought about the encounter, the more I was convinced that *angel* was the only explanation that made any sense.

A week later Lena and I set out for another trip to upper Maryland to visit Lena's dying friend. My car, of course. It seemed I dodged the same chugholes on I-95, and we stopped at the same restaurant for coffee and a chicken burger. We chose a non-smokers' table for four off in an isolated alcove. As we often do, we laid our purses—my black vinyl and her black leather—on the empty chairs next to us and kept talking. Our conversation had returned to the topic of angels, especially our mystery mechanic.

I told her my son's view. "God sure must have a good sense of human nature. He allowed both of us to see the kind of person we would most easily trust. You would take to someone dressed in a jacket and tie. I would be at ease with someone in jeans." I added an opinion of my own, "And God must also have a good sense of angelic humor."

As we were talking, all alone in this section, a big, unkempt man walked in. Unkempt by any standards: shoes untied, a belt presumably hidden under his overriding belly, which wasn't quite covered by his dirty shirt or worn jeans.

I can't say with certainty that this man was up to no good. And I'm not sure why I didn't say anything to him. I just watched as he walked behind and toward the chair on which Lena had set her purse. He was close enough that she sensed his presence. Our conversation halted.

Suddenly, the man stopped abruptly, as if he'd walked into a wall. After a second's hesitation, he turned as if to leave the room. He took three or four steps toward the door, then pivoted around and came back, heading straight for Lena's things.

By this time he was right behind her. Though his hands were hidden from my view, by his stance he appeared to reach out for her bag. But he jumped back, as if he had touched a live wire. Then he jumped again and again, as if being shocked repeatedly. And shock is what I saw on his face.

That man was out of there fast.

Knowing he was gone and hearing my short version of what I'd seen, Lena smiled. "Well, thank the Lord."

"Yes, thank the Lord," I concurred, raising my eyes toward heaven.

Back in Texas we learned an old hymn,

> *Blest be the tie that binds*
> *Our hearts in Christian love;*
> *The fellowship of kindred minds*
> *Is like to that above.*

People could claim that Lena and I are not "of kindred minds." On some counts, I'd agree, but the older we get—and we're both beyond the famed three score years and ten—the tighter God pulls that "tie that binds" our fellowship based on Christian and sisterly love.

In recent months, we sisters have had more in common than ever. We've added angels to the list of subjects we *naturally* talk about when we're together.

Our messengers may come in different attire, but we both agree that they're with us. Watching. Protecting. Demonstrating that God's love is of the personal variety, tailored to our unique personalities.

❧ Virginia Sendor ❧

"MY JEWISH UPBRINGING WAS NOT A RELIGIOUS ONE," Virginia Sendor tells you in the article that follows. "Nevertheless, I sensed that I had undergone a deeply spiritual experience." The experience she refers to happened in 1960, during a time when a terrible illness threatened to take her life. In many ways Virginia's is a classic case in which most of the ingredients associated with angelic encounters are represented—brilliant white light, music, and what Virginia describes as "the graceful profile of a being with shoulder-length hair." Yet there is more: an out-of-body occurrence so powerful in its effect that Virginia dedicated the rest of her life to helping those who are dying.

Virginia has spent years providing counseling and hospice care in an effort to soften pain and to show that death is but a natural part of life. She has gone back to college to work toward an M.P.A. in health administration. She is a consultant and advocate in gerontology with strong convictions about "age-ing to sage-ing," the wisdom acquired by the old to be given to the young. She founded and became executive director of a New York State-certified hospice for terminally ill patients and their families. Sadly, lack of funds, and the freezing of state funds in particular, caused her to close the hospice doors in December 1991. Even so, her work has proven to be a catalyst for a number of hospice programs to be found on Long Island today.

Obviously, Virginia is a woman with a deep social commitment. Born in the Bronx ("back in the trolley car days"), she went to high school there and graduated from Hunter College in Manhattan. She has always felt that a meeting with Eleanor Roosevelt was a turning point in her life; it strengthened her determination to work for the good of the community. That she was honored as "1991 Woman of the Year in Health Care" in her own Long Island community is but one indication of her achievements and the respect that friends and neighbors have for her.

The Sendors—Virginia and Bernard—have lived in Westbury, Long Island, for over forty years. They raised their two children there, a son and a daughter, and now they are grandparents. Bernie has worked all of his life in the field of graphic arts, particularly binding and printing at his own firm, Sendor Bindery, in Manhattan. The Sendors both love opera and ballet. It seems fitting that Virginia should smile when she tells you of her great fondness for Humperdinck's *Hansel and Gretel,* "especially the end of Act One when the angels gather around the children as they lie asleep in the forest."

What does it mean to Virginia to have seen an angel? Just a whole, quieting approach to life, that's all.

"It means peace, bliss, joy," she says, "an expansion of the heart. In the midst of all the craziness in the world it keeps me grounded." She goes on to talk about "that beautiful, special light" and the "presence" she can almost reach out and touch. "Later, when I had a bout with cancer, I refused to worry—and I survived. When I travel, when I take a plane or check in at a hotel, I feel protected. Driving in a car, I know my angels are with me. Yes, my angels are always with me."

Seeing the Light

by Virginia Sendor

*The poor man died and was
carried by the angels to
Abraham's bosom.*

—Luke 16:22 (RSV)

N THE LATE 1970S, a chain of deaths—my mother's, a younger brother's, a close aunt's—left me utterly grief-stricken and despairing. If only I had used my time with Mama more wisely during her last days! Did she and Richard and Aunt Julia ever know how much I really loved them? Was there anything they had wanted to tell me before they died, but I never gave them a chance?

Despite my professional background in rehabilitation counseling, I was haunted by painful feelings and questions. I decided to enroll in a graduate workshop on "Counseling for Death, Dying and Bereavement" at Hofstra University in Hempstead, New York. And it was in that class, on a frosty January morning in 1981, that I came to terms with a mysterious event in my life.

The professor began talking, in a matter-of-fact voice, about something she called "near-death experiences." Such experiences, she stressed, were so well documented that there was even a worldwide group devoted to them called the International Association for Near-Death Studies, Inc.

My thoughts whirled. Could this professor be talking about the same sort of experience I'd had twenty-one years before? An experience so real, yet so bizarre, that I'd never told a soul about it? A rush of long-held-back memories flooded by mind. It seemed like yesterday.

It was spring 1960. I'd learned to live with a severe hearing impairment that had affected me since childhood, and I'd even earned a master's degree in special education, majoring in rehabilitation counseling. But I was very ill. The news from my doctor was devastating: acute uremic poisoning with complications. He said I had three to six months to live.

At first, I didn't have the courage to reveal this prognosis to my husband Bernie. When I told my mother, she urged that I be treated at a special clinic in Texas run by a doctor she trusted. She offered to help take care of my children, ages three and six, while I was away. So I traveled to Dr. Herbert Shelton's clinic in San Antonio, Texas. Mama and Dad took the children, and since money was tight, Bernie stayed home to work.

The clinic, in an isolated area far from the downtown and residential areas of San Antonio, was surrounded by the scrubby Texas brushland and mile upon mile of open sky. I fully expected to die there. After about three months of following a strict vegetarian diet and drinking nothing but pure water and juices, I seemed to be getting worse. I was very weak. The thought of dying frightened me, but I was so ill that I almost began to welcome death to be free from pain.

And then, on a clear September day, the most extraordinary thing happened. I left my body on the bed and was hovering up by the ceiling of my room. And then—I was outside the building. I had no more pain and was no longer aware of my body. Below me and around me was a panoramic view of the vast Texas landscape and the horizon. I seemed to be at one with the universe. I had no sense of time or space.

Next I became aware of sounds that I hadn't been able to hear without my hearing aid since I was a little girl. And what I heard was the most beautiful music—an ethereal blend of sounds, so natural as to surround me, envelop me. In addition to the music, I heard some words—the same phrase chanted over and over again. I didn't know the language, yet it was strangely familiar.

I floated and seemed to be beyond the horizon, and then in the distance appeared the graceful profile of a being with shoulder-length hair. It was a blazing silhouette from the waist up and glowing with its own most beautiful brilliant-white light. Like the music, this light seemed to surround me, envelop me, shine right through me. Although it was white, it seemed to possess all the colors of the rainbow, like the light that radiates from a perfectly cut diamond.

I was filled with a sense of wholeness and peace unlike anything I'd ever known. "The Light" I experienced was love, pure and unconditional—the "something more" that I'd yearned for since I was a child.

Now, with crystal clarity, came these word: *"Baruch Atah Adonai...Baruch Atah Adonai."* They were woven like a golden thread through the beautiful music that surrounded me. *"...Baruch Atah Adonai."* I had no idea what the words meant.

Then I was back in my room again, in my bed. I felt weak and racked with pain. My chest felt crushed, I couldn't breathe. And there was something terribly wrong with my left side. Dr. Shelton and some attendants crowded around my bed.

Later on, I learned I had suffered an angina attack, but I would be all right. My left side was palsied, but months of intensive physical therapy enabled me to regain the use of my arm and leg; gradually, my overall health improved.

Three months later, in December 1960, I was able to go home.

Though I am Jewish, I wasn't brought up in a religious home. Nevertheless, I sensed that I had undergone a deeply spiritual experience, something too meaningful to risk being ridiculed or diminished in any way. So I told no one, not even Bernie, about "The Light." I felt protective. The experience was too deeply personal to be shared at that time.

Then, twenty-one years later, while sitting in a college classroom with the nurturing support of about twelve of my peers, I felt a powerful sense of affirmation; I began to see a connection between the deaths that had led me to attend this class and my own near-death experience. It was an awakening.

I completed the course and plunged into advanced studies on death, dying and bereavement. Meanwhile, I solved the puzzle of those words I'd heard. They had sounded vaguely familiar, like Hebrew, so I made an appointment with the rabbi of our local synagogue.

I met with him several days later in his paneled office and told him about my experience and the words. I was sharing what happened for the first time—and I felt as if it had just occurred. "Rabbi," I said, "it was many years ago that I heard those words. What do they mean?"

He looked at me intently. *"Baruch Atah Adonai,"* repeated the rabbi softly, stroking his chin, "means 'Blessed art Thou, O Lord.'" I gasped and repeated, *"Baruch Atah Adonai*—Blessed art Thou, O Lord." How appropriate!

Blessed art Thou, O Lord. So many nights as I drifted off to sleep, dog-tired from studying, I felt my strength and well-being restored as I recalled the magnificent "Light," the beautiful music, the reverent words.

Over the next year, I found myself increasingly drawn toward the study and practice of hospice care and counseling to help terminally ill patients and their loved ones. At the heart of hospice philosophy is understanding death as a natural part of life, an experience not to be shied away from or denied, but met with confidence and hope. The idea is to improve the quality of the life remaining to the patient and not to prolong the dying process.

Recalling Mama's, Richard's and Aunt Julia's drawn-out battles with cancer, I understood the hospice belief that, while pain control is always necessary, in some cases a course of radical surgery or the use of heroic measures or extended therapy with drugs, chemicals and radiation may not be the best use of the time the dying patent has left.

Healing can occur on many levels, and it may not always mean a physical cure. The dying person is often in need of deep emotional and spiritual healing as well. And so is the family. "You can't learn everything about hospice work from books," explained a dear friend who is a clinical-oncology nurse specialist. "You need to be able to listen at a different level, intuitively, so you can respond to the unspoken needs of dying patients and their families and friends."

Listen at a different level. That was one thing I knew I could do after nearly half a century of living with a severe hearing loss. Many times I'd watched a person say one thing with his lips, while his eyes and face and body communicated an altogether different message.

On Christmas day, 1981, I was nearing the end of a double shift as a volunteer in the hospice unit of one of our local hospitals. One of the patients was a middle-aged man dying of cancer; he had been hospitalized for a period of time and had become comatose.

The medical community generally agrees that, even when comatose, the patient is aware—however dimly and mysteriously—of the presence of others, aware not only of their presence, but also aware of what they are saying and doing. I explained this to the man's wife and two grown daughters as they stood in painful silence outside his room.

"He knows you're here," I said. "He knows it's Christmas day. Come into the

263

room. Say his name. Talk to him. Share your love for him. He *will* hear you." I asked his wife, her face drawn with exhaustion and grief, to stroke her husband's cheek. "Kiss his forehead," I whispered.

Death was imminent, and the man's extremities were cold and turning blue. I asked one of the daughters to take her father's hand into her own. "Hold it tightly with both of your hands," I said.

I asked the other daughter to cradle her father's feet. "Cup them in your hands and massage them gently," I said. "Stroke his toes, his ankle...there, give him some of your warmth and life...."

Then I stepped aside, over to the window. I joined the family in my mind and spirit, praying that healing would take place where it was needed, in whatever form that might be.

I saw the man's toes start to move just the tiniest bit. And then a bit more. His color began improving.

"Look!" exclaimed the daughter at his side. "He's beginning to move!"

Then the man's eyes opened wide. He was not disoriented in any way, as might be expected considering his critical condition. Clear and bright, his eyes shone with joy, reflecting love. He was aware of all that was going on around him.

Before leaving the room to allow the family time alone. I encouraged them to share their deepest feelings with him. "Now is your chance to complete any unfinished business you may have with one another. Now is the time to talk about love—to say words you always wanted to say but never had time to—or to ask forgiveness."

As I left, I realized that my own pain about Mama, Richard and Aunt Julia had been eased by helping this family.

And when I returned some three-quarters of an hour later, I saw something that took my breath away. For present in that patient's room were not only the patient and his family—*but "The Light" was there, too!* Filling the room with a glorious radiance, shining in our eyes, *"The Light" was with us!*

My hospice work has taught me that in this life, along with the joy, are pain, sorrow, suffering, death. But through it all, God cares. He is light—*"The Light."* And when God's Light breaks through our darkness, it is with a power strong enough to redeem even the most hopeless-seeming situation—even death itself. To me death is not hopeless. It is not the end.

Baruch Atah Adonai!

⮈ Sandy Letizia ⮊

SANDY LETIZIA HAS WRITTEN A LOVE STORY with a bittersweet ending. It would probably never make a movie, even with its fascinating element of mystery, because its characters and setting are not exotic. It's about a good, solid, middle-American family who love one another, go to church regularly, study their Bible, and care for their neighbors. It is simply all too normal for Hollywood.

Sandy and David Letizia were married for thirty-six years, and had spent most of their lives in and around Mansfield, Ohio. They had known each other since high school, though Dave was two classes ahead of her and they didn't date until his junior year at Ashland College. Dave was an athlete, and when he became a teacher, first in Mt. Gilead, then in Clear Fork High School near their home in Bellville, he was a coach and athletic director. Meanwhile, except for a brief period when the Letizias invested in a soft ice cream operation that mostly she ran, Sandy stayed home to be a mother to her two sons and daughter. She was also a den mother, a homeroom mother, a cookie baker, and an indefatigable member of the school play audience.

One day in 1973, a neighbor lent Sandy a videotape about guardian angels that had a surprising effect on her. She and Dave were every-Sunday church-going Presbyterians, and for years they had belonged to Bible study groups where they took what they learned very seriously. In all those years, Sandy realized, she'd been reading about God's angels, but she'd never thought about them as being real. Maybe real then, back in Bible days, but not real today.

I wonder if I could have a guardian angel, she thought to herself. At first she was amused at the idea. *If I do, I'll call her Susie Sunshine.* No sooner had that name entered her mind than something spoke to her: "No, not Susie Sunshine—Felicity." Sandy was bewildered, still is, as to how that name, such an unfamiliar one at that, had come to her. Looking back, she figures that this little guardian angel interlude happened only a few months before the angelic event you will encounter in her story.

Sandy is a widow now, and she continues to live in the same house in the woods that she and Dave bought over thirty years ago. The mothering she does these days is *grand*mothering. She keeps herself on tap for one of the eight groups that make up a local, twenty-four-hour prayer chain. In her Bible studies she goes on searching for what God intends for her day by day, but there is one spiritual point that she doesn't have to ponder: No longer does she think that angels were only active in the ancient days of the Bible.

Something Wonderful Is Going to Happen

by *Sandy Letizia*

*Wait on the Lord: be of good courage, and he shall strengthen
thine heart: wait, I say, on the Lord.*

—Psalm 27:14 (KJV)

 OMETIMES, EARLY IN OUR MARRIAGE, for no reason at all, my husband would stop at a flower shop and buy me a dozen roses.

"A whole dozen!" I'd say, overwhelmed and aghast. "Oh, Dave, they're too expensive. We can't afford this."

For a while he didn't hear me. If he saw twelve roses, he'd buy them all. To the Italian romantic, more was better.

But finally, my Scotch-Irish nature got through to him. "Oh, Dave, they're so wonderful—but I just can't appreciate more than one at a time."

Soon he was coming home and handing me a single rose. "For you," he'd say as he planted a kiss on my lips. Eventually, he settled on one rose in particular, an unusual lavender rose that I always gushed over: A sweet, powerful fragrance wafted from its delicate petals.

The longer we were married, the more often he stopped at the florist—for a rose. Or sometimes he bought three, which we both justified by saying that each represented one of our three children.

One day late in August 1993, after thirty-six years of marriage, he brought me three red roses, presented with an apology: "I'm sorry they're not the lavender ones. They didn't have any today." No matter.

I usually enjoyed the flowers while they lasted and then threw them away. I don't know why, but those three red buds I set aside to dry whole, before the petals fell off. Below the rose hips I clipped the stems; then I laid the blossoms in a heart-shaped dish on top of the living room TV, where they still sit.

Ours was a marriage that got better with age—and after being tested by some dark days. In March 1973, Dave, the thirty-seven-year-old athletic director and all-purpose coach at Clear Fork High School, suffered his first major heart attack. When he went back to school in September, he still had a teaching job, but someone had decided to relieve him of his coaching responsibilities.

Over the next twenty-one years, I lost track of how many times I drove him to the emergency room of Mansfield General in Mansfield, Ohio. In addition to numerous heart catheterizations, he had open heart surgery, and eventually they put in a pacemaker. But doctors never did really control the angina attacks with pain that split through his chest as if it were torn open with a knife.

And for several years right before his doctor prescribed retirement from teaching at age forty-eight, Dave lost control of his emotional pain. Dave's physical stamina had been the core of his identity—as football player, as a lifeguard honored for saving a child's life, as the eighteen-year-old "hero" who pushed his buddy out of a fiery gas explosion, as an athletic coach. And as that physical stamina slipped, he dulled the pain with drink.

This was not the Dave I knew and loved, but a moody, argumentative, unpredictable stranger. At night I would cry myself to sleep, silently praying *God, where are You? What's happening to us? Please make it better.*

But, of course, Dave had to make his own decision to "make it better." And with great courage, he admitted himself to a local alcohol treatment center.

He walked out of that hospital a changed man. Just one bit of evidence? That first night home he sat on our bed and said, "Honey, from now on I'd like for us to join hands and pray together at bedtime." Pray together? This would be a new venture, but I was willing, even eager. And that night I prayed, "Lord, thank You for giving Dave back—now better than ever."

Walking with new inner strength, Dave was able to face his early retirement in 1984. With time on his hands, he turned his talents toward serving others. He looked after his ailing mother. He was treasurer of the board of a local hospital.

But often his acts of mercy were the random variety: He would drive someone to medical treatments or the airport. We frequently visited a former student who'd been shot and paralyzed on the job as a policeman. He liked to send anonymous cashier's checks to people in hard straits. He was the Good Samaritan type who would stop if he saw a car accident. The first-aid kit in our car trunk was as much for strangers as for ourselves. About the only limit to his generous nature was an agreement we had: We did not pick up hitchhikers. No way. Too dangerous. You never knew who might force you to do what.

There was a second fresh aspect to Dave's retirement years. Always aware of the precarious nature of his health, we valued every minute we had together. When weather permitted, this meant spending the afternoon at Sun Valley pool, open to members and their guests. We had a regular pool pattern: We would swim a few laps, then we would lounge over in the corner mostly by ourselves. If I'd found an interesting book or magazine, I'd read aloud to Dave, who would listen while catching his rays. He enjoyed the sun. But with some vanity, he also hoped a good tan would conceal the gray pallor that came with his heart condition.

We also attended a weekly Bible study, and that's where a friend pointed out Psalm 27:14 (KJV): "Wait on the Lord: be of good courage, and he shall strengthen thine heart: wait, I say, on the Lord."

"I felt as if this verse was for you, Dave," she said. Dave and I latched on to the verse, though the two of us saw slightly different meanings in its promise. We both agreed that "strengthen" meant "heal." But I was sure God meant to repair Dave's physical heart. Dave, on the other hand, sat me down on the couch one day and said, "Sandy, you know that this heart ailment is someday going to be for keeps. Listen, I want you to remember that when I go to heaven, I'll receive the ultimate healing—no more pain! Please promise me you'll remember that and try to be happy for me."

Don't say it! Don't say it! That afternoon I cried and clung to his chest, wishing he hadn't admitted what I didn't want to hear. *No. God was going to heal his heart. Heal his heart. Soon. Very soon.*

On Wednesday, September 1, 1993, around noon, Dave and I headed for Sun Valley pool. This day we had broken our usual routine in that we'd taken two cars. When we left the pool about three, I turned left and drove directly home; he turned right, toward Mansfield, intending to drop in briefly at his sister's.

I'd been home for about an hour when Dave pulled his Oldsmobile into the garage. As he walked into the family room, I knew something was wrong. His "Hi, hon" was always followed by a kiss or a hug. But he just stood near the door, no smile, no warmth.

Oh, no, not again, his heart, I thought. "What's wrong? Are you in pain?"

"No, that's not it at all," he said as he sat on the couch. "I just had the strangest thing happen. On my way to Margaret's I saw this hitchhiker. A well-dressed black man."

"You didn't pick him up, did you?"

"Yeah, I did."

"Dave, you know our agreement about picking up strangers. It's just too dangerous."

"I know," he said apologetically. "But *twice* something told me to pick him up. It was important. I just *had* to. How often have you seen a black man with blue eyes? This guy had *intense* blue eyes."

Dave obviously needed to talk and I let him.

"I asked him where he needed to go. He said, 'Just drive for a while and I'll tell you when to let me off. Normally, I wouldn't be out today, but my boss has a special job for me to do.' After a mile or two of comfortable silence, the guy said, 'You know St. Stephen?' Then I thought I'd picked up some kook.

"I answered, 'No, I don't think so.'

"The guy insisted, 'Oh, yes, you *do* know St. Stephen.'

"I decided this was no one to disagree with, so I played along. 'Well, maybe I do know him.'

"When we got near the corner of Cook Road and Main Street, he said that's where he wanted to get out. I offered to take him farther, but he said no.

"So I stopped the car, and the guy reached over and squeezed my hand. He looked me straight in the eye. You've never seen such *beautiful* blue eyes. He said, 'Very soon something wonderful is going to happen to you.'

"That was weird enough, but I know I didn't hear the car door slam when he got out. And when I looked in the rearview mirror and around to the right and left of the car, he wasn't there.

"So what do you make of all that?" he asked, still utterly bemused.

273

It didn't make any sense at all unless… "Dave, I think you've seen an angel."

He looked startled. "Think so?" He thought a minute and said, "I don't know much about St. Stephen. Do you?"

Having attended weekly Bible studies for years, we both felt somewhat biblically literate. But for Stephen we drew a blank.

"I think I'll call Mary Jo," Dave said. "She'll know." Our neighbor Mary Jo was a devout Catholic. Dave figured she would be familiar with anyone in the "saint" category.

I listened again as Dave told Mary Jo his story. I couldn't hear what she said, but suddenly Dave's eyes got real big. He turned toward me and said, "I can't believe it. That's what my wife just said."

I burst out laughing. Mary Jo's analysis confirmed mine; she thought he'd seen an angel.

Mary Jo knew that Stephen was a New Testament martyr, stoned to death. "I'll dig up some more information about him and get back to you," she said.

That night, at a meeting, I told three friends the story. Each wondered aloud what "wonderful" future Dave had in store.

For two or three days the angel and his message occupied our thoughts. Dave was pensive, reflective, in outer space, as a kid might say. What wonder might this be?

Then over Labor Day weekend, we went to a picnic at the home of friends we'd had since college days. We got further distracted with earthly matters when Dave had to spend a night in the hospital for observation of chest pain they said wasn't heart-related. The hitchhiker faded from the picture, at least in my mind. Mary Jo didn't call with additional information. I didn't look up the Bible story. St. Stephen might as well have never entered our lives.

But on Friday morning, September 10, the racking chest pain once again sent us to the hospital. By one o'clock we were in the emergency room. Doctors and nurses hovered over Dave. He was begging for relief and perspiring as if he were a saturated sponge. His hand clutched at his chest as if he were trying to pull out the pain.

Though the sight was intolerable to me, we'd been here before. I'd repeatedly heard the doctor say the same words: "Sandy, things don't look good. You'd better have your children come."

I called my children, and then for a long time—too long—Dave and I were left alone. I rubbed his back, held his hand. To try to focus my mind on God and not on the horror of Dave grasping at his chest, I pulled from my purse a devotional booklet and started to read.

At one point, after nurses had come back in, David gave a desperate prayer: "God, how many times do I have to go through this?"

I just held on to his hand, until he soon yelled out and lurched onto his side. Immediately, someone grabbed my shoulders and ushered me away from the bed; buzzers went off and the curtains closed.

Dave had come around so many times in the past, I couldn't believe the doctor's five-o'clock words: "Sandy, there was nothing we could do. Dave's gone."

"I want to go, too," I blurted. Without him at my side, I didn't want to stick around even one hour.

But I did. I lingered one hour. Two hours. One day. Two days. I greeted more than five hundred people at the funeral parlor, many of them Dave's former students, each sharing a heartening "Mr. Letizia" story.

The day after the funeral, our neighbor Mary Jo came over to visit. Sitting next to me on the living room couch, she listened as I therapeutically rehashed the events of the last week.

I had a long list of "what ifs." "What if the doctors had paid more attention?

What if I had pleaded with God to spare Dave's life, instead of sitting there reading a devotional? What if we'd gone to the heart specialist in Columbus earlier in the week?..."

Mary Jo interrupted and reminded me of her phone conversation with Dave two weeks earlier. "Don't you see?" she said. "The angel was trying to tell Dave that he would soon be going to heaven."

The hitchhiker. An angel. *Very soon something wonderful is going to happen.*

It took another week for the words to sink in. At our next meeting, my women's Bible study group gathered around my grief. Before we looked at our assigned Scripture, I told them about the hitchhiker, about his message, and the mystery of St. Stephen.

The group leader insisted, "Well, right now, let's read the story of Stephen." As we went around the table taking turns reading portions of the story, God removed the blinders from my eyes. In the first days of the Christian church, Stephen was one of seven men chosen for the particular task of helping the needy, especially the widows. He was the first Christian martyr, and minutes before his death, Stephen turned his face toward the sky and said, "Look...I see heaven open and the Son of Man standing at the right hand of God" (Acts 7:56, NIV).

Jesus stood to welcome Servant Stephen into heaven just as Jesus had welcomed Servant Dave. The thought sent goose bumps down my arms. When I connected the hitchhiker's prophetic words of "something wonderful" with St. Stephen's heavenly vision, my haunting "what ifs" washed away with a torrent of tears.

Though only fifty-eight years old, Dave had died in God's good timing.

I tried to hold on to the angel's message and also to Dave's own warning to me, which now was a comfort: "I want you to remember that when I go to heaven, I'll receive the ultimate healing—no more pain! Please promise me you'll remember that and try to be happy for me."

No matter what scriptural or personal assurances you rely on, there's only one way to face the death of a beloved spouse of thirty-six years: one day at a time.

Every morning I awoke and repeated a prayer, begging God for another measure of joy, some small grace that would heal a bit—as the Scottish would say—of my breaking heart. Some daily grace got me through the autumn and winter. And soon I was well through the spring—and dreading the dawn of June 1, our wedding anniversary.

One morning late in May, my friend Joan called. Did I want to join her and another friend, JoAnne, on a spur-of-the-moment drive to the Kingwood mansion and gardens in Mansfield?

Why not? The sky was sunny, a perfect day; getting out would be good for me. I'd meet them at the rose gardens, heavy with their first burst of brilliant blossoms.

"Look at this one. And *this* one!" We'd lean down to smell a red, then a pink or yellow or white variety, each seeming more fragrant and carefully crafted than the last.

Out of the corner of my eye, I suddenly spotted a lavender blossom that drew me away from my friends and down a solitary path. As I savored the velvet petals and the sweet aroma, I retreated into a private world: at home one day when Dave walked in, saying, "Hi, hon, I'm home. Here, I bought you one of your favorite lavender roses. For you!" I wished back the tender moments of my marriage, and then glanced at the identifying marker. What was the rose named? *Angel Face.*

As healing tears again washed over my cheeks, I looked up into the cloudless sky. "O Lord, thank You for this lavish measure of joy. And Dave—thank you, honey, for the roses. All of them—even these."

When I had composed myself, I told my friends about Dave's Angel Face roses.

The garden grief turned to laughter as we walked to our cars. "God and Dave make quite a team," said Joan.

I finished the thought: "Working together to deliver joy. To the widows—like St. Stephen. And through the face of angel roses."

> *Care thou for mine whom I must leave behind;*
> *Care that they know who 'tis for them takes care;*
> *Thy present patience help them still to bear;*
> *Lord, keep them clearing, growing, heart and mind;*
> *In one thy oneness us together bind;*
> *Last earthly prayer with which to thee I cling—*
> *Grant that, save love, we owe not anything.*
>
> —George MacDonald

∽ A NOTE FROM THE EDITORS ∽

All Night, All Day, Angels Watching Over Me was created by the book division of the company that publishes *Guideposts*, a monthly magazine filled with true stories of people's adventures in faith.

We also publish *Angels on Earth*, a magazine of true angel stories that is sold on the newsstand. It's also available by subscription. And subscribing is easy. All you have to do is write to Guideposts, 39 Seminary Hill Road, Carmel, New York 10512.